COLLECTED
POEMS

ALSO BY JEET THAYIL

POETRY
These Errors Are Correct (2008)
English (2004)
Apocalypso (1997)
Gemini (1992; two-poet volume)

AS EDITOR
The Bloodaxe Book of Contemporary Indian Poets (2008)
Divided Time: India and the End of Diaspora (2006)
Vox2: Seven Stories (1997)

FICTION
Narcopolis (2012)

JEET THAYIL
COLLECTED POEMS

ALEPH

ALEPH

ALEPH BOOK COMPANY
An independent publishing firm
promoted by *Rupa Publications India*

First published in India in 2015 by
Aleph Book Company
7/16 Ansari Road, Daryaganj
New Delhi 110002

Copyright © Jeet Thayil 2015

All rights reserved.

No part of this publication may be reproduced,
transmitted, or stored in a retrieval system, in
any form or by any means, without permission
in writing from Aleph Book Company.

ISBN: 978-93-84067-43-4

1 3 5 7 9 10 8 6 4 2

Printed and bound in India by
Parksons Graphics Pvt. Ltd., Mumbai

This book is sold subject to the condition that
it shall not, by way of trade or otherwise, be
lent, resold, hired out, or otherwise circulated
without the publisher's prior consent in any
form of binding or cover other than that in
which it is published.

This book is for my parents,
Ammu George and TJS George

Contents

Preface xv

NEW AND UNCOLLECTED POEMS (2003-2015)

Declaration of Intent	3
Imaginary Translation	4
Future Watercolour	6
Incantora the Impossible	7
Separation	8
Separation's Sonnet	9
Suicide's Sonnet	10
Every Dead Girl is the Death of the World	11
Hell Hath No Puri	12
Untitled	13
Rules for Citizens	14
What Would You Know?	15
Boyhood	16
Autological	18
The Consolations of Age	19
Dear Editor,	20
Tomorrow, Tomorrow	21
The Book of Me	22
Found Poem	23
53 Views of Abstraction, 1 Rhyme, 0 Blackbirds	24
Ghazal	26
The Mothers	27
Life Sentence	28
The Haunts	29
Re: Application	32
Again by Water	
I THE BOOK OF BRUCE	33
II MY AMNESIA	35
III MY LIFE WITH THE PRESIDENT	37
The Future Infinitives	39
Still Life with Insomnia	40

The Reckoning	41
Three Versions of Rilke	42
Dear Salil,	44
Interview with an Alien	45
The Jump	47
from *The Book of Chocolate Saints*	
Saint Mummy	48
Saint Santosh	49
Saint Nayantara	50
Saint Mathai	51
Saint Gandu	52
Saint Goonda	53
Saint Gandhi	54
Saint Maurice	55
Saint Erasmus	56
Saint Moses	57
Saint Augustine	58
Saint Antony	59
Saint Josephine	60
Saint Martin	61
Saint Nicholas,	62
Saint Pelagia	63

THESE ERRORS ARE CORRECT (2008)

Not Remembering	67
Poem with Prediction	72
Blue Ghazal	73
Premonition	
1. Gone and *gone* doesn't mean a thing—	74
2. In the hands of the priest	75
3. Sunday holds its head	76
4. Among the trees of the city,	77
5. To see if I'd still be here,	78
6. To leave me on the F train, a lone	79
7. to lick the meat from each other's bones	80
8. To our bodies, expanding, numberless, slow,	81

9. Forget the sea, let it fade	82
10. When it rains, the dead descend, you appear,	83
Flowers for a Parijat	84
After	86
The Annotated Gita	87
To Baudelaire	88
The Heroin Sestina	89
Malayalam's Ghazal	91
Spiritus Mundi	92
Letter from a Mughal Emperor, 2006	94
The Two Thousands	96
A History of Religion	97
Cut to Bits by the Sickle Moon	99
Why Should You Believe Me?	100
The Origin of Remorse	101
Wagah	102
War is Work	103
View from the Ground	105
Two Interventions	106
Nativism	107
Superpower	109
The Sonneteer	110
The Parrot of Happiness	111
The Miniature	112
Against Gravity	113
Dear Heptanesia,	114
The New Island	115
Aquatic	116
Verticality	117
Dietary Habits in the Mountains	121
The Cook's Tale	122
My Lie	125
My Paris	126
Migration	127
Gabreel in America	128

Late Vespers at the Hudson
  1. UNTITLED   129
  2. A CURE   130
  3. SUBLINGUAL   131
  4. RECOVERY, PARTIAL   132
  5. STEP EIGHT   133
  6. UNTITLED   134
  7. UNTITLED   135
  8. LATE VESPERS AT THE HUDSON   136
In the City of Insomnia   137
Grand Central, 2003   138
You are Here   139
Flight   141
The Penitent   143
Quiet and Concerned with Provenance   144
Big Yellow Music, Like   145
The Eye   146
The Opposite of Nostalgia   147
New Year, Goa   148
On Taking a Line for a Walk   149
After Brodsky   150
The Art of Seduction   151
Sonnets for the Mouth   152
For Agha Shahid Ali   156
2007   157
A Home for the Holidays   159

ENGLISH (2004)
I MOVEABLE
About the Author   163
Moveable   165
Skewed   167
Afloat, the Immigrant Martyr Elect   168
It Wasn't Until the Lawyer Told Me I   169
The Man Who Married Water   170
September 10, 2001   172

II SHAPESHIFTER

How to Be a Girl	173
How to Be a Toad	175
How to Be a Leaf	176
How to Be a Horse	177
How to Be a Crow	178
How to Be a Bandicoot	179
How to Be a Krait	180

III ACHE

Fool and Flea	181
The Air There is Crowded	182
Botero's Pear	184
Villanelle with a Line from Baudelaire	185
There's a Chinese Wall Between Us	186
Sailor's Log	187
Psalm Secular	188

IV THE GENESIS GODOWN

English	189
Summer	192
Moon	193
Monsoon	194
Dawn	195
Winter	196
My Grandmother's Funeral	197

V ACHE

The Other Thing	198
Meanwhile, Over in Orissa	199
The Brown Nude	200
The Boredom Artist	201
Portrait of the Artist as an Old God	202
Elegiac	203
He Do the Husband	204

VI SHAPESHIFTER

Heroination	205
The Unauthorized Autobiography of Rain	207
Ophelia	208
Inventory	209
Yet Another Mother Poem	210
At Kabul Zoo, the Lion	211
Slumming in Bombay, Beelzebub	213

VII MOVEABLE

Land's End	214
Pashupatinath	215
Kovalam	216
Imaginary Homecoming	217
London	219
Doune	221
Hongkong, 1997	223

APOCALYPSO (1997)

Working Girl	227
The Quilt	229
Ballerina	230
Apocalypso	231
Betray Me Before I Betray You	233
Pushkin Knew Heaven (*A Place Where Nothing Happens*)	234
Hello Goodbye	235
His Twin is No Hypocrite	236
Where This One Came From	237
Vertigo	239
The Adulteress Addresses Herself	240
One Morning at the Cattle Fair	241
Genesis Partner	242
Wedding Picture	243
Self-Portrait	244
This Mortal	245
Tentative Like Us	246

Other People's Deaths	247
I, Chatterbox	249
Falling	250
Daft Sermon	251
The Guru	252
Letter to America	253
Blueprint, Bombay	254
No More Tears No More	255
Jacob's Circle	256
Family Affair	258
Horse Breakfast	259
Trout Fishing at Night	260
Life Lessons	261
The Mercy Tree	262

GEMINI (1992)

What You Are	267
House of Silence	268
Writing in English	269
Our Lady Speaks	270
Fixing Father	271
Oneroid	272
Log	273
With Women Other Than	274
A Morning Prayer	275
Her Song	276
The Lover	277
The Body's Betrayal Sung Out in Song	278
The Alcoholic at Dawn	279
Praise the Nod	280
Hymn to Him	281
A Circular Song	282
Acknowledgements & Notes	283
Index of first lines	287

Preface

I was born the year Billie Holiday died, in 1959. In my recurring dream of Billie, she is a photo on the front page of a newspaper that prints only obituaries. It's a dream stolen from a poem called 'The Day Lady Died' but that doesn't make it any less strange. Someone sent me a photo of Billie, in which she's leaning into a microphone, her face swollen. There's a red whisky tone on her skin and she seems to have nodded out standing, though you can't be sure because cat's eye sunglasses are obscuring her eyes. I put the photo on my desk and that night my usual dream of Billie was replaced by another: Billie and Roberto Bolaño smoking smack in a Parsi sanatorium on Bandra Bandstand. When dawn lit up the dirty sea and shit-stained rocks and crowds of morning strollers, Billie was sitting cross-legged in front of a candle, a ripped seam of burnt foil in her hand. A matchstick burned in her slender fingers and a strand of fresh seaweed was entangled in her hair. As Billie's head finally touched the floor, Bolaño got to his feet and gathered his briefcase. He told me that the sun was high and soon it would be too hot to walk or work. 'Only poetry is not shit,' he said. 'Stop wasting so much time.' Even in the dream I realized that this was a fairly accurate rendering of my writing career. I've written four books of poems, two libretti, and one novel. The thousands of pieces of indifferent or bad journalism do not count since I wrote them for money. The poetry books are out of print, but that is as it should be if you're an Indian poet writing in English. The libretti were privately printed, which means they were never in print in the first place. The novel, *Narcopolis* (2012), in which I tried to write of Bombay as a city of violence and intoxication, is the only thing I've written that remains in print; again, this is business as usual for an Indian poet. Considering my modest oeuvre and how little of it is available, it's an odd and oddly gratifying sensation to put the four books of poetry together in this volume, along with some new poems and poems that were written many years ago but never published. While compiling it, I left some poems unchanged, some I discarded, and some I rewrote, because, among poets, the rewrite tradition is an honourable one. As an example, here is a poem from

Apocalypso, followed by the new version, in which Kafka makes an unannounced late entrance:

SELF-PORTRAIT (1)

He likes the stark symmetry of this place;
nothing excess, nothing wasted,
each book in its nook, slotted in.
(Unhappiness is something
altogether ambivalent:
Do you want to be happy,
he asks himself periodically,
or do you want to write?)

Now he lifts saucepan to stove,
images atone forever in his hands.
Ghosts of celebrations past
throw themselves lemming-like
into the insufficient flame.
Each small act is attended
by a whole host of demons,
friendly and not.

At nightfall, exhausted by toil,
he falls instantly into
a dreamless, honest sleep,
open to the elements.

SELF-PORTRAIT (2)

Unhappiness is a kind of yoga, he tells himself
each morning, a breath meditation; besides,
do you want to be happy or do you want to write?
When he lifts saucepan to stove, images atone
forever in his hands. Ghosts of celebrations past
throw themselves lemming-like into the meagre
flame, each small act attended by a host of demons,
friendly and not. The world is code, smoke signals the
dead have left us to decipher, knowing we cannot.

At nightfall, exhausted by toil, he falls deep into the
dreamless light changes, the dead or dying sea.
A mountain moves and nobody notices. The world
is old and set in its ways, and K. is saying, Of course
there's hope, there's always hope, but not for us.

I want to say, at this point, that it is difficult to ignore the posthumous nature of a preface such as this. It is usually a task left to others, preferably after the poet's death. In my case, there are circumstances that make this writing inevitable. *These Errors Are Correct* (2008), written in dedication to my wife, who died, is the last full-length collection of poems I intend to publish. For various reasons, I am unable to equal the poems in that book and it seems to me that if you cannot equal or improve on your last book, it is better not to publish at all. I am fifty-five years old. Time, once a friend, is now the enemy. Each day is a gift that must be returned. I live in a rented house in a large Indian city. The thick air is alive with chemicals. Chaos is my friend and closest neighbour. This is my life and these are my collected poems. There is nothing collected about any of it.

NEW AND UNCOLLECTED POEMS
(2003-2015)

Declaration of Intent

Your lips go from sunny side to suicide in a single click.
You're too fast for any sniper.
You know when to hit the ground and stay down.
When you step out, armies rise up or die by your eyes.
Your soldiers are of all ages, genders and religious denominations.
They have nothing in common but the image of you
carried in secret lockets, or burned into their third, unblinking eyes,
or tattooed into armpit and hairline and between the toes.
If you glance at yourself when you're kissed, the mirror plucks out its eyes,
for no other image will ever again suffice.
You are kissed and kissed again. You are always kissed.
You wake up to a kiss and fall asleep to one. In between, kisses.
You say your dreams in a stunned small voice
that belongs to the other world.
Your pauses are glacial, the age melds its continent to your breath,
your tears are the end of seasons.
Sometimes, on an escalator, if you speak to yourself
your unheard words will make a stranger stop in grief.
Your power is sustainable and biodegradable.
Your green will outlast plastic.
You invented electricity. The grids belong to you.
They blaze your praises, visible from rocket ship and satellite.
When you skip town, the wind on the street says your name.
Ah, it says. Kang. Sha.
No one escapes your influence.
Once, out of my mind, I tried, but the grass barred my way.
And the stars wandered out of their pens.
And God exhaled.
And no faith was left in the world.

Imaginary Translation

The Hermans dance a white concertina
in the bordello of the flagrant kulcha.
Even if the Hermans eat rice with Jesus
they will die, obscure as roses.
If you were here you'd be coming
to the sound of castanets. You'd be a flower
on the floor. Meanwhile, spreadeagled
above, softly afloat, you again,
the better you, lost in a welter
of images, or a wind that blows
all night in the dry streets of the city

in which we drag our feet to dawn,
followed by trumpets or love,
broken elevators or cell phones,
broken songs, broken
membranes and minds and smoke,
the broken introduction to a species,
broken zygotes without malice,
broken axis of the rooster's eye,
where stupidity & the devil dwell.
Will you return to the assembly of roses?
Do you know why the night is huge,
beyond consolation or embrace?

Even if the Hermans eat rice with Christ
they will die in the obscurity of roses.
The Hermans dance a white line
between white concertina & gallows,
in the bordello of fragrant kulchas.
If you were here you'd come to the sound of
castanets, you'd be Homer pissing
in the wind, encased in ornate symbols,
and floating above you, softly floating,
who else but you, Ana, who knows

the smell of castanets,

smell of sawdust varnish sun?
Do you, Ana Rossetti, love each
petal's sour breath as I do?
How quickly the sweet misadventure
passed, youth's diversions,
turbulence, precipitatory tremblings
in the penumbra of pubis,
the Hermans with their solitary wars,
old bordellos of secondary kulcha,
white concertinas floating above
us, flagrant, lost, O Hermans, O love.

Future Watercolour

The black cars huddle on the street and
settle in for the night.

One day we'll leave this place. The cars
will trumpet after us.

Goodbye, beasts, street. Goodbye, me, you.
Hello, new ruin.

What then? Years later in Berlin, you will
return as the wounded

flesh of a pear on my bedside table.

Incantora the Impossible

is experienced in the collection
of praise. In her prized hands

perspiration is fuel, food for humans,
symmetry the supreme accomplishment.

What blue streaks, mermaid shimmies,
dolphin style on brilliant water.

The white bird creaks in the trees
of the sea. Of what does she speak?

What distant fados or diminuendos,
what longing screes?

Her words are vowelous and few,
but when she sings, she sings of you.

Separation

Town of ghosts, where I or some other breathes
the black unchangeable estrangement.
Your perfume fades from dead white sheets,
from pillow cupboard my dead hands.

Only a whisper remains and this too will fade,
forget me.

No rain returns from the dead earth.
No message returns.
How much dust and distance between us?
Brightness fades with memory.

Separation's Sonnet

What are you doing, what improvised thing?
In a borrowed room your cell phone rings,
each ring measures the floor, the rungs
of your dream. Holding, I ask how you sing,
and for whom. To imagine the bed you're in,
the vertiginous smile that will break him,
the man whose roses bleed at your window.
To want is to wait, as I do in the place I know,
my breathing loud and single as the room,
its smell of spider dust and old perfume.
Each small thing lasts longer than the shiver
that is life. I fix the remembered instant:
you on your feet, singing, shaking a river
of salt from our shared overheating skin.

Suicide's Sonnet

Like someone who comes home late
to find the furniture rearranged,
I'm stepping lightly on my paws
but there's no one here to waken.
O captain, my captain, mistress, chatelaine,
objects had a way of breaking
in the life we shared. For example, China
from, where was it, Ecuador?
But never mind the wry disclaimers,
why did you dismantle the fire alarums?
Why does the night sweat the sheets?
Why is the kitchen full of weaponry?
Why do I return, now more than ever,
to the window high above the street?

Every Dead Girl is the Death of the World
[Fragment]

The lynx with the deep pink eyes
drops a rose on the girl's pink lips
rough tongue licks and dips
then he shivers in his thighs and dies

The girl whose eyes are red
strokes the red welt on her skin
strokes the soft red within
and says, it's I who should be dead

The girl whose skin is blue
sees the world's one blue eye
sees you from a thousand miles high
and says, I'm here I see you be true

Hell Hath No Puri

It was stacked against us from the start.
The Puris, those witches, needed man-
bhaji. I made the mistake of bedding one,

I'm not sure which of them it was,
and because I'd had one, all three saw me
as common property. My music was good.

Better than ever, as a matter of fact.
That was the worst of their lies.
My music reached them, it always did.

Sun streamed through the windows,
breakfast steamed on the table, Bel Puri's
rat's tails dipped into her oats, fork

frozen in mid-air, worms unfrozen.
I brought the last line home
so slow you could put your fist through

the notes, no words, just a long vowel
like the wind's, like regret or longing.
They couldn't bear the idea of love.

I didn't look back, that too is a lie.
(I didn't need to. I knew she was there.)
She did not turn, her eyes were on me.

They pulled her down from jealousy.
How she howled when they took her.
I have no reason to lie. I have no body.

Untitled

the future was as they said it would be
but they didn't mention incontinence
or retched tongue taste of bile
reflux taste of deepest entrails
new ash taste on the breeze

didn't mention it didn't know
the way skin puckers at sunrise
rictus grin at night didn't know
or carefully omitted to tell us
how long the black cloud the road

Rules for Citizens

1. Let us govern those who undertake the telling of stories.
2. Censorship is good governance. Self-censorship is an attribute of the highest civilization.
3. If an actor speaks of God, he will be chastised. He will be refused an encore. If he repeats the speech, he will have his licence revoked.
4. Let us govern those who undertake praise of the next world, since what they say is neither true nor useful to us.
5. Our best recourse is to be warlike.
6. We do not deny that storytellers are good at their job and give people what they like to hear. But the better they are, the less we wish our children and men to hear them.
7. We shall refute their attempts to be wise. We shall scoff when they repeat their vile allegation, *Whereof one cannot speak, thereof one must remain silent.*
8. We will do away with the dirges of famous men and leave them for women, and not the best among women either.
9. Let us abolish those fearful and terrific names, Cocytos, the River of Lamentations, Styx, the River of Fear, Ganga, the River of Death in Life, Lethe, the River of Bliss, Tigris, the River of Affliction.
10. We shall disallow travel and the mingling of songs.

What Would You Know?

'About suffering they were never wrong,
the old masters.' Oh shut up, why don't you,
you old bastard? I've had it up to here
with your opportunistic philosophizing,
you who've never suffered but for your art,
who wouldn't know a liver from a heart,
shut up, I can hear you. If you weren't so
white and creased and vegetable, I'd give
you a hearing, but here you go, no,
now fuck off, old master poet, old fart.

Boyhood

All are agreed he was sly about his needs.
When the daily ordeal of prayer was done,
he went on: his prayers had just begun.
But when his father stepped out,
the boy took the book and posed with it
in the mirror above the sink, his eyebrows
knotted into one. His soul, some said, yearned
to sink into a bowl of ecumenical blood.
What he dreaded were holidays and weekends,
his father home, the house silent. He dreamed of
flight, of silver-bodied Boeings that sailed the
skies like battleships, silent beings from
elsewhere, he at the controls, silent too, raining
cotton candy on the stupefied. Undecided
about God—who he is, what he wants—he knew
fear, not love. He wanted obedience, not choice.
More than the blood he drew from the
neighbourhood's cats—each lasting longer
than the one before, injured where no one saw—
he loved the servants who cleaned and
cooked, loved the smell, the hawk and spit,
the blasphemy of it. When the old cook
washed himself in the servants' bathroom,
he'd wait outside for the man to appear
in a towel. Cleansed, he breathed the deep
odour of carbolic sweat and Dettol.
He loved disorder, the chaos of rain pounding
on the town, the flooded roads. At thirteen,
his father prone in the back of the ambulance,
his mother wild, he let panic thrill and encircle him.
He heard cartoon voices in the next room
and trained himself not to move, trained his
eyes in the mirror to be flat, to withhold news.
At the beach he sat away from his relatives.
When children's voices echoed from the water,

the water whose genius trembled in the sun,
he heard not children, but the cries of the doomed,
and lifting his head saw men women babies,
bodies aloft, lifting downward like
butterflies from the towers of the world.

Autological

From this window,
other windows,
lives squared in
neat parcels,
growing slowly
visible, nightlights
pinked by dawn,
in moments, in minutes,
to you, you
alone, all these
praises, every
blessing, the manic
gleesome gnats of
gold, mandibles
gnashing, streaking
the street in sticky
blonde juice,
until each grid
irradiates sun's
yellow business,
who brings the day,
who brings the light,
O King,
the light you give us,
the permission you give,
so we may transform
ourselves in flight,
great gears
above us meshed,
great engines
under whose wheels
everything glows.

The Consolations of Age

Dear Editor,

Two reasons I like writing sonnets—
and why two, why not fourteen
reasons, the shape compact and clean
on the page, why not, since we're on it?
Well, one, I like the way it leads
you by the hand down the stair
of the page, leaves you resting on air
as on an armchair, while someone reads
to you the words you want to own.
Two, I want to say something about bliss.
I like bliss, and if I had to narrow it down
to a couplet, I'd narrow it down to this:
You start with a line and follow it through,
the sonnet writes the sonnet, not you.

Tomorrow, Tomorrow

you remember cities never seen
twisty minarets or a
quarter where impressionist sunshine
squares coiled cobra
alley, silver glitter, bridges, sighs

to follow one horizon is insularity
flesh inert, spirit unwilling
blindfold vision's narrow sky
mind-wasted crumbed linen
the afternoon's madeleine tea

the world's a day away
your old suitcase waits as dawn
roses the brickwork and a cab
black suited driver honking
sidles like a hearse to the curb

The Book of Me

Out of the depths, O Lord, I cry to thee:
Lord, hear thou the voice of me!
Be attentive; and if thou canst not be attentive,
be tolerant of the endless span of my lament.
Put down, O Lord; Lord, put down the book
of my transgressions. Where does it begin?
Where end? Who will withstand
its rigour? Who answer the daily taint
of inquisition? Who survive?

Unsettled, O Lord, in a trough,
day deferred, then denied,
impaled I am upon thy yellow antlers,
never to arise, not in this life.
What feasts have we forgone, what
nights without tincture of your breath,
to paw the air and offer my belly for
priests to police their terrible tithe?
Gross guardians, I bow down.

Found Poem

The Lord is my shepherd, I shall not want.
He makes me lie down

in still waters.
He leads me to green pastures.

He restores my soul and helps me walk
in the path of righteousness, for his own sake.

And, yea, though I walk in the valley
of the shadow of death I shall fear no evil. He

comforts me with staff and rod,
provides me with wine and bread.

In the presence of mine enemy
goodness and mercy enter me.

You anoint me with oil, my cup
overflows. You lift me up.

53 Views of Abstraction, 1 Rhyme, 0 Blackbirds

1. In a red and blue swatch of sky
2. The only moving thing was I,
3. And a kite of three minds.
4. One was made of fire,
5. One of ice,
6. The third mind was made of cumuli.
7. A spun metal kite
8. Made ON 5/6/78 (not 79)
9. Was no small part of the pantomime;
10. It was the play entire.
11. In a map of the high
12. World, Osip, the only clear sign
13. Was the fat unshy
14. Cockroach on Stalin's smile.
15. I ask, Why?
16. You reply,
17. The lords will tire
18. Of misrule. We must bide
19. Our time.
20. The dish, of Parsi Spiced
21. Stir-Fried
22. Squid, serves 4 or 5.
23. I do not know which to desire,
24. The red name or, aiie,
25. The blue. Aye,
26. Or the yellow room where names are cried.
27. The interlocking tri-
28. Angle and two tied
29. Circles are one. The woman is a find.
30. I don't care how much, she's mine.
31. She points to the sun, which shines
32. In red and yellow smears, in lines
33. Of fine
34. Yellow and red, and indigo dye
35. That fills my

36. Line of sight.
37. Are these specks or birds that fly
38. In formation, a crazy Y?
39. O Vengeful, thy
40. Eyes are dry.
41. Thou leavest us with a sign
42. And a question, Which is nigh:
43. The beauty of the succubi
44. Or the beauty of the lie?
45. Thou, as wise
46. One, or as Love Crucified?
47. Hi,
48. Shakti, it's New Year's Eve, 2007, 5.49
49. p.m. We're in a coffee shop in Manali and I'm
50. Looking at the ice
51. On the Himalayas and writing this line.
52. I have no idea at the time
53. But in three months to the day you will die.

Ghazal

When you leave you'll take what I remember of love.
Summer will feel like the December of love.

From forest fire to flicker in a matter of weeks,
What will be left but an ember of love?

Paper money's no good in some parts of town.
They take only the (soiled) tender of love.

Banish the moon and stars, delete the music.
What else remains to dismember of love?

Never mind your unguent, your obscure remedy.
No antidote exists for the distemper of love.

Your eyes of no colour, like the sea at 4 a.m.
My eyes are red, or is it the umber of love?

Your nose, Jeet! This isn't Edam, Cheddar or Brie.
Such ripeness marks the Camembert of love.

The Mothers

Some are cute and old,
others are brave and bold.
Mine is dead and cold.
She judges me with eyes of gold,
and though her eyes cannot hold
mine, they move in search
of me each night. How you lurch
backward in time to fold
me back into your lonely perch
where no egg will hatch.

with Shakti Bhatt

Life Sentence

Let's say you're not opposed to the ghost
in principle, you understand her neediness,
and let's say she's distracted, or busy,
she's busy looking for a way back in,
but the shore appears distant,
not to mention, impossible to attain,
a far-off place where her former friends
no longer speak her name, which is lost,
and no word she hears is audible
through the static and the clatter;
so let's say you forget to speak her name,
you do not repeat her lovely name,
because your talk is of meat and money,
and let's say you're not crazy or bitter,
it's just that you don't want to hear her say,
Why, why did you not look after me?

The Haunts

As starlight, as ash or rain,
as a smear on the moon,

as a tree, say a champakali,

as a leaf or a man impersonating a leaf
torn into shreds
and fed to the wind,

as the smell of a small dead animal,

as a tremble on the stair,
a mouse or air,
a tear, a heave,

as fear glimpsed from the window of a plane,

as a telepathic ginger cat
a slit of moonlight
that enters the locked house
and leaves its stinking spoor in each locked room,

as a boat on the Muvattupuzha about to drop
its load of two children and a woman
into the monsoon current,
and if the river had taken them
how much pain would it have made,
how much would it have saved?

as my mother trying to push the monstrous head out from
    between her legs,

as the stalker at 4 a.m.
swing creaking in the park near my house
downturned face white in cell phone light,

as the god that swaggers the top floor of my spirit

or the ghost that twists in the basement
or the slave that inhabits the middle,

as an inconsolable soprano nearing the end of Ave Maria,

as a cherry red Stratocaster Elite
found in a pawnshop in Vancouver
and bargained down to eight hundred dollars,

as bad heroin in a Delhi alley
pink pill crushed up and sold in a twist of paper
snorted hungrily for no pleasure,

as a woman (again and again)
whose hair curls, mouth moves or eyes well like yours,

as a figure by the side of the Expressway
urging me to crash the car
in a voice so calm and wise
it took every shred of sanity not to give in,

as good heroin in Zurich,

as a bloated white face on the ceiling of a borrowed room
talking to me all night
in words I am too high to understand,

as a violin creeping through the
trees in front of Humboldt University
and I understood music as the hunger
that eats those it stokes,

as the careful lizard that patrols my brain,

as the dazzled bird who steals—gems, junk,
whatever comes—to build
and what did I build but a house of dust?

as a ritual between newlywed insects

as an insect, horned shivering convulsed
tiny tyrannosaurus throes,

as the white of my beard, whiteness beyond snow or stupor,

as the abandoned child you were
who said goodbye to wind and water
stepped into the opposite of air
said no to earth-blood

said stop to body-blood
arrived as white shadow
without features or desire
as a drop of sacrificial oil

made your atoms integrate
tumbling dripping under
in your hurry to enter
the kingdom of eternal life,

as illness, as liver disease
and the river of red wine that cures it,

as the black grape that made the wine,

as a black burn on the leg that appears overnight and stays for years,
as an unexplainable lump on the shoulder,

as the sound of someone close crying softly in the night,

as a dead girl with blood-red lips
blood-red eyes and cheeks
blood-red wrung neck,
as crematorium smell of
camphor and meat,

as whatever you want,

just come back.

Re: Application

1. The organism's structure centres exclusively on eating and excretion. These contradictory impulses may explain test subject's anxiety, invocation of regional deities and general bewilderment.
2. The breathing mechanism is subject to frequent breakdowns. Too much depends on the regular flow of air to the lungs. The rudimentary blood network and the single heart require immediate redesign.
3. The organism needs simultaneous adjustments with regard to visual stimuli, tenderness, narrative cohesion and sexual information. Constant maintenance is unjustifiable with regard to cost effectiveness.
4. Elevational ability is absent and the desire for it is all-consuming. The subject wants to fly but is unable to stay aloft for any significant length of time. As a result, it is the location of tremendous psychic conflict.
5. The greatest drawback is its pathological craving for certainty; there is no doubt among us that this condition is related to its overall emotional neediness.
6. We must mention, too, its vulnerability to weather, its susceptibility to time, and its nightly rest requirements.
7. Overall, our consensus is that the organism is exceedingly disappointing, not to mention banal.

NB: We wonder if these flaws are prefabricated elements of the overall design, due not to incompetence, as has been alleged, but as a study in staged obsolescence. If so, we are prepared to consider the possibility of allowing the project to continue in its current unsatisfactory format.

Again by Water

I
THE BOOK OF BRUCE

I set out as soon as we made landfall. I took only water, my sketchbook, a box of paints. I wanted to be on my own. I wasn't looking for adventure—I'll tell you that much straight off the bat.

I climbed up through the brush with my pack swinging against my side and soon I came to a village. Put it this way, one minute I'm stumbling up a hillside and the next I'm stumbling into a huddle of huts, cookfires going for dinner, smoke rising into the trees. I'm looking at a bunch of faces looking back at me.

They took me to the headman, whose name was Bruce. He wasn't happy to see me. He was busy conducting the evening prayer, chanting to a pair of bus tickets and an old copy of *Time*. (Everybody prayed twice a day, at twelve hour intervals. Each family had its own gods—this was a strict rule—gods that could not be interchanged or cross-worshipped. Bruce and his family worshipped paper.)

Bruce got up off his knees. He welcomed me and asked me to be seated. Then, going to the family shrine, he pointed out his favourites, in order.

1. Currency notes, mostly euros, rials and rupees. No dollars.

2. Expired prescriptions for unavailable medication, written in a sloping hand: *Opium Tincture* .... 3. *Absinthe Balm for Neuralgia*. Etc. They were nailed to the wall above the bed.

3. A page from Larousse's French-English dictionary.

4. Toffee wrappers.

5. A calendar of Asian birds, with colour plates of the Brahminy kite, the Bustard and the Bee-eater. There was a faded printout stapled to February.

Statistically Improbable Phrases: peninsular juxtaposition, evergreen biotope, black mesial stripe, tank margins, cognitive trespass, black wing quills, gentle interrogation, mixed heronries, remarkably obliterative.

6. Several pages from a biology textbook (with illustrations of the reproductive cycle of freshwater fish).

9. A napkin from Wendy's with a line drawing in blue ballpoint of a woman whose legs were so long her head seemed to be growing out of her hips. She was riding a missile powered by a submarine propeller. There was a phone number, 9872437766, and an initial, S.

Bruce was happy to show me the family gods, and though he didn't insist that I join in the prayer—a low chanting punctuated by percussive yelps—I could tell he was hoping I would. I didn't of course. Taking sides in local disputes, debates, or religious bonhomie is strictly forbidden to the crew of the Ark.

Instead, I showed Bruce a snapshot of my wife and son. Big mistake: he wanted it. He installed it right away, on a shelf above the front door. I'm sure it's still there, a picture of my wife and son eating chocolate ice cream from a blue bowl. Then he noticed my sketchbook and I had to give that to him as well.

There was a special prayer service to welcome the additions to the family pantheon.

Afterwards I took a tour of the village. Bruce's immediate neighbours worshipped an empty bottle of Lancôme perfume and a muddy shoe, the mud lovingly incorporated into the shrine. A family worshipped copper utensils and plastic bags; another worshipped a mouse, which it fed and bathed and called Fred. An extended family of bald men and dreadlocked women worshipped prosthetics and rubber tubing.

A family whose hut was at the outskirts of the village—they were unpopular—worshipped nothing at all. They said their god was invisible.

I would have liked to see more, but it was getting dark and I was expected back on the Ark. Since I'd given Bruce worship gifts the other families said they too wanted a keepsake of some sort. I left the paints, a tin box with evenly spaced circles of colour. Bruce divided the pigments among the villagers. Each family got a colour, and there were some left over.

Colour was their newest god and the most mysterious.

II
MY AMNESIA

They were fighting fish, no question about it, so brilliantly coloured and so numerous in the freshwater pool that I stood dreaming there for a long time. I roused myself when it got dark—I had to return to the Ark. But I took the fish with me, two small ones in a clear plastic bag, and I put them in a tank in the banquet room.

We had a great number of fish when the Ark set out, including rare specimens of *Toulouse Tyrannasaura* (dwarf dinosaur fish that mated for life), *Masonica Chameleo* (secretive pack fish that disguised themselves as other fish), *Al Jeebira* (Saudi Arabian counting fish), and my favourites, *Cannibalista Sologo* (small fish that lived alone and ate themselves from the inside out). Our years of travel had depleted them. We were forced to eat the big fish when the Ark encountered torrid zones and none were left but a pair of spiny Inquisitor fish and a dozen tiny Communion fish, which resembled goldfish but refused food unless they could eat en masse. It was a fraught coincidence that the Inquisitors and the Communions found themselves together: the Inquisitors were hated by all fish for their aggression and fanaticism, and the Communions were pitied for their timidity and fearful nature.

I ask myself how it was that I first took a sip of the water in the tank. I'd noticed the change in the fish of course, it was impossible not to. Days after the arrival of the mysterious new fighting fish, the Inquisitors gave up their relentless spying; and the Communions began to go for long solitary swims, to lose interest in eating together, and to fight among themselves for the most negligible reasons. It was as if the fish had forgotten their essential natures.

As I say, I don't know what made me try the water, but I did, I took a sip and the effect was immediate—a draining away of residue and a sense of ease. For an hour, I forgot everything: my youth, the name of the town in which I'd lived when the earth was dry, the terrible trouble that had put me on the Ark, sailing without hope of real landfall. And when the effect of the water passed I was refreshed, energized, as if I'd slept a long dreamless sleep.

One morning we found a piece of floating land—there were many in that hemisphere—and we stopped. I set up a tank with the pair of fish and a hand painted sign.

MIRACLE AMNESIA FISH—YOU'LL FORGET EVERYTHING

I exchanged cups of amnesia water for fresh vegetables, fruit, clothing, oil, whatever was available. Soon I had more provisions than I needed, but the people kept coming. Pillars of society, charlatans, householders, fools, they'd come back for another drink as soon as the effects of the first had worn off. Some would fall asleep near the tank, leaving only when they had nothing more to trade or when I asked them to go. If I didn't keep an eye on them, they would steal draughts of the water. They lost interest in maintaining the engines of their lives.

The women blamed me for turning the men into amnesia addicts, but soon they joined in, living from one drink to the next. When I became bored by the tedium, the cycle of blame and shame, I weighed anchor and set sail. I'd stop somewhere new and set up the tank. However long the voyage, I'd watch the amnesia fish, whom I named Love and Fame. It helped me pass the time.

III
MY LIFE WITH THE PRESIDENT

He was stacking branches for firewood in neat rows. He wore a battered cowboy hat. I went up to him and blurted it out. He said, Okay, but we sleep in separate beds.

The place wasn't much. A house and a barn in a brush clearing: no way to find it but to look for smoke at dawn. I'd hear it in my head, something enormous, a big body of water, and I'd look around. No water.

He was a good man, a good provider. You couldn't rely on him to keep his word, or to be around in a crisis. But he was kind to me.

On the first night, I woke up drowning. I was choking on air. He took me by the hand and led me to his altar. He prostrated himself, said I should do the same. He was praying to a picture of that hot actor who played Conan the Barbarian.

He prayed to pinups, Arnold, Sly, Justin, Enrique, and guys I'd never heard of, Charles Atlas, Johnny Weismuller? I supposed it was normal enough. People worship stones wood the sun a river. I told him I worshipped shoes myself. How far will a colour poster of a muscular guy take you on a hot day on a long road?

He had no books or newspapers. He wasn't allowed to bring any with him. Besides, he'd only ever read the Bible, the King James Version, and 24 issues of the *National Geographic*.

Under his pillow was a road map of Baghdad, well-thumbed.

He liked to talk, mostly about automobiles, weather patterns, horses, clothing trends, television programming, hospitals, the salaries of public servants, the methodology of torture. But his conversation always ended in the same place. He said, The reason the people of this region mix sugar in their food is to compensate for the taste of the water. You must have noticed it, kind of dry and metallic. This is desert country. Very few trees. Absence of water: absence of paper.

He blamed the Imams for everything.

I woke one day and found him praying in a language I'd never heard. He was sitting at his desk with his hands together, staring at a poster of a man with a large shaved skull. He was so loud I joined in. I said the first thing that came to my head. *The American retailer H. Gordon Selfridge coined the phrases, Only—— shopping days until Christmas, and, The customer is always right.* He didn't react.

He prayed for three days. He forgot to eat and sleep. I kept checking that he hadn't forgotten to breathe.

I don't know how else to put it. He got old. He got old all of a sudden. He spent more time at home. He said he wanted to be surrounded by 'collaborators and students.' But to tell the truth we were bums, vagabonds, young men out to see the world.

One by one the others left, until there was no one else, just me. When he knew he was going, he let me kiss him. I knew he was going because he let me kiss him. He hated to be kissed on the mouth.

The Future Infinitives

All over those bland, continuous
states, in ghettos amalgamated beyond
Sikh, Muslim, Hindu to one easy race-
name, South Asian, one umbrella brand,
Indian-American, in basement sublets, dorms,
mortgaged cookie cut homes
where god lights blare like truck horns,
coatless or bundled, hardhat headscarf
askew in cold sun, a mother and daughter
slaughter ready at the register, or that
man, rushed, clenched shut at Dunkin' Donuts,
at Apna Bazar Cash and Carry, on Roosevelt,
a food-fragrant driver of a yellow taxi,
those sisters, shy and not shy, rival
sports trophies and photos arrayed,
the dead one's husband, emperor-sized
bed against uncurtained white wife light,
empty house and he alone with remote,
& the priests of the convention cathedrals,
limp wrists extended over wine cocktails,
suits and flesh glossy in the gloaming,
wild glint of fossil fuel, DC's far domes
winking yellow, oh all over those blonde,
bland states, saying to Gauri's camera,
It's me, barefoot in the ballroom of the dream,
poised, posed, alone, almost American.

for Gauri Gill's 'The Americans'

Still Life with Insomnia

The moon endures its own revolving,
the star its nonexistent light.

A flower blooms purple in a loved one's throat.
So much endures and means nothing.

We who wait where the sky descends—
only we do not endure.

We drop. We disappear.
It ends

with a squeal of brakes and fright in
the night, our eyes wide to let the light in.

What does he see
when he looks down into the blue,

his work snagged like light in a tree?
Is he ashamed?

Frailties that hide in the day define us
from outside in, quietly rich, almost

swirling, not ready to be named.
The moon endures your secret weeping.

I'm not awake, I dream of sleeping.

with Jennifer Dorr & Dave Dorr

The Reckoning

She woke early and read a sura about the Day of Terrors,
the Day of Severance, the Day of the Inevitable,
when one blast shall be blown on the trumpet,
and the earth and the mountains shall be upheaved
and crushed into dust at a single crushing,
and the woe that must come suddenly shall suddenly
come. On that day, she read, ye shall be brought before Him,
and he whose book is given to him in his right hand shall say
to his friends, Take ye it and read: such is my reckoning.
But he whose book is given in his left hand shall say,
Oh that my book had never been given me, and that I
had never known my reckoning. She thought,
I know in which hand my book will be given to me.

So when the phone rang, she heard the sea, or something
like the sea crashing against the apartment's high
windows, and lifted her hands to the light and watched for the
tremor, and remembered a shred from the morning's tumult
and said, What one misses about love is the yielding.
I miss the yielding, Kamala said, and put down the phone.
And in a week, or less, in five days or four, she was gone.

for Kamala Das

Three Versions of Rilke

1
A DAY IN AUTUMN

Lord, it's time for summer to end.
Stretch the shade across the old clock's face,
push the wind hard into the treeline
and hurry your fruits into ripeness.
Give them two more days filled with sun,
and let a late sweetness take the bough.
Let the moment last until it's done.
Who has no home will not build now,
who is alone will be alone always,
staying up to read, write, and stall
his return to the park's green avenues
when the leaves begin at last to fall.

2
THE DEAD

He knew of death what all men say
that those it takes away
do not return.
When she too was taken from his sight
into something more than night,
and he knew that she was gone,
her kindness and her laughter gone,
then all at once he understood,
through her, the dead,
and went with them,
and did not listen to what they said,
and listened only for her tread.

3
AUTUMNAL

Leaves fall,
as though, far
above, the trees are
turning bare.

Each day the earth
falls further
from each star.
We too are

falling. Only
one is not, whose
two hands hold the
world in place.

Dear Salil,

Good to hear from you tonight on the worldwide web.
I've been ill and wishing a blight on the worldwide web.

But your triple haiku, like medicine, lifted me enough
To respond in kind, here, right on the world wide web.

For I too am taken by it, the bittersweet honey and gall
Of the ghazal, its whisper and bite on the worldwide web.

If the sonnet is an English rose, the ghazal is Arab,
hooves moving at the speed of light on the worldwide web.

And the haiku? Delicacy, precision, delight, and more:
It provides light cross-cultural insight on the worldwide web.

A ghazal in response to a haiku in response to a sonnet,
Jeet, what are you spoiling for, a fight on the worldwide web?

Interview with an Alien

The first episode
arrived 'full-blown, clear as water,
with such a rush I couldn't avert it.'
You said the morning dissolved

into something you had no name for
and you left the room in a panic,
the future running at you haywire,
in images, your head epiphanic,
or just sick.

*My mind slipped a notch,
I lost myself.*
Payback, I'd say, for the Scotch,
the pills, and whatever else
was swimming in your system
at the time.

What we wish to examine
is the assertion
at the heart of your account, re:
your mind fell out of America,
back to *the sweet country*.
Did you think such a
claim would escape our attention?

We questioned your wife, the au pair,
the critics, the fans, and we wonder
what you were thinking, you,
an educated man, blaming
the tutelar spirit who populated you, stuffed you

with kindred needs for sex, alcohol, art,
blaming the hand
of god for everything, sky the colour of blood,

flowers that smelled of fear,
sea like a dirty carpet on the sand,
and the thing that left you wired, poisoned,
the wasted hours,

the rooms you slept in. I
do not say 'lived in,'
for I too am an educated man.
The difference? In your case education
is an affliction.
You cannot stay.

The Jump

It's going to take one line or six
to remake this poem

from a declarative sentence
in couplets to something

that takes you to Africa,
where the ant

lion waits
       in tall grass,
              ready to jump

into the clean white field of this page.

from *The Book of Chocolate Saints*

Saint Mummy

the Astonishing, climbed trees & buildings;
hid in ovens or cupboards; could not abide
people, for she smelled sin inside;
loved knives, wept, ate all manner of things;

led the dead to purgatory, then paradise;
let herself be dragged under water; loved tombs;
held fire & son without harm in her arms;
holy woman touched of god; given to ecstasies;

seeker of souls in extremis; hunter of devils,
or flatly insane; in-womb maker of insane
son, whose company of saints
she rebuked; garotted herself for thrills.

Saint Santosh

of small fry, pi-dogs & romancers;
perfected the whistle to bring them home;
untroubled by Rome;
pecked to death by the breasts of dancers;

enjoyer of denim & rhythm;
drowned star of the Republic of Kerala;
whose motto, Kiss My Posterior,
was repeated by graffito, lore & drum.

Saint Nayantara

mother of Rooturaj the ulcerous,
mended his leggings; served Foruitus
her husband, adulterous,
whose curses were precise & numerous

& repeated by reputable servants;
washed husband & son with her tears;
crucified at dawn by municipal spears
cast by her own strong hands.

Saint Mathai

of tailors, convenor of abusants;
preacher of licks & mortifications,
poor man's vexations, fornications;
scourge of children & parents;

fell into light in the diocese of Mahim;
cooked for the accountant of Dongres;
one with the hungry, condoler to compadres;
quartered on the tracks at Panjim.

Saint Gandu

of varied climes in the same location;
singer of hymns; consoler of women;
arpeggist to monsoon; firestarter repentant;
exiled to the precinct of Garadulistan,

where he learned the art of toadying;
called asshole & cunt too many times to mention;
gave it up to a warden in juvenile detention;
disembowelled by order of goading.

Saint Goonda

of Byculla, started his career
as overseer of security for usurers;
promoted to treasurer,
but rivals poisoned the boss's ear;

jailed from cowardice;
saw false gods approach on cricket night;
asked refuge of Hindu & Hottentot;
strangled by friends at the Great Gate of Peace.

Saint Gandhi

of Porbunder; in darker South Africa,
saw the light when travelling by train;
wore only homespun;
gave up salt & sex; so tragic a

man, who would split a nation
in two; befriended apocalypse;
died with the name of God on his lips;
shot by a man with God in his name.

Saint Maurice

or Moritz, or Moorish, or Mauritius,
upper Egyptian third-century legionary;
canonized early, before the Holy See
reserved that right to the Pope's sole hands;

turned white in early representation;
a thousand years later, painted as he was,
black soldier, black saint; patron of weavers,
swordsmiths, dyers & infantrymen.

Saint Erasmus

or Erasmo, or Rushmore, or Elmo;
bishop, Syrian; fled persecution
to hide as hermit in the Lebanon;
caught, tortured, made to tell more,

his tongue cleaved to the odd bell
of his mouth; rolled in pitch,
set alight, saddle-stitched
by flame; rescued by young angels.

Saint Moses

the Black; Ethiopian servant,
lost in Egypt; criminal, but no master;
wandered & plundered &, at last, a
fit subject for conversion;

inevitable, but dangerous;
gave up crime; to God gave thanks;
joined a group of desert monks;
murdered by marauding Berbers.

Saint Augustine

of Hippo; educated son of a pagan
father; driven by appetite & ambition;
had an African concubine & son
at age twenty; restless man, theologian,

who loved comfort & women & pondering
on God; hear me, he cried, who is trembling
in the darkness, & stretch forth thy hand,
recall me from my wandering,

let me be chaste, Lord, but not today,
for today there's she & she & she;
in old age, restored to himself & to thee,
he wrote the Confessions, read to this day.

Saint Antony

of Egypt; born in Coma
to Christians; at twenty,
his parents died & left him plenty;
he gave it away; summered

two decades alone in the desert;
then: followers, a garden, baskets;
patron of weavers, domestic animals, pets;
healer of those poisoned by the ergot.

Saint Josephine

of Darfur; stolen
at age nine
by traders from Araby;
sold in Khartoum;
sold & bought
so many times
she lost her name;

someone gave her
one: Bakhita
the fortunate, a little
joke between
men who travelled
hard; but the name
stayed, as did Josephine;

sold to an Italian,
who gave her to another,
who shipped her to Venice;
joined the Canossians;
took her vows;
died with Oh,
Madonna! on her lips.

Saint Martin

de Porres; born in Lima,
one of two bastards;
father, a Spanish knight,
mother, a freed black
slave; apprenticed at twelve
to a barber-surgeon from whom
he learned to tend the sick;
established hospital & orphanage;
welcomed African slaves
on arrival in Lima; animals
loved him, as did the poor
& powerless; patron of mixed
races, social justice,
(Italian) barbers & hairdressers.

Saint Nicholas,

or Sinter Klaas, in the Dutch vernacular;
Americanized to Santa by settlers;

born in Turkey, not the North Pole;
patron of brides & unmarried girls,

travellers, sailors, children & Russians;
made ruddy & fat in representations;

life story lost, found as Christmas father;
of reindeer, the master.

Saint Pelagia

the Penitent; or, the Harlot of Antioch,
whose disgraceful profession was actress,
beauty & wealth her transgressions,
unforgivable to those who had neither;
she paraded on the promenade dressed
in finery, trailed always by a
retinue of admirers & the hot scent of
musk; one evening, she passed a
group of bishops who turned their
backs on her, all but Nonnus of
Edessa, who paused in his preaching to
admire her, a woman successful in her
profession & he had failed his flock;
troubled by admiration, he prayed
all night & at first light went to cathedral;
Pelagia followed. What then, what
conversion, repentance, denouement?
She gave away her finery & spent
the rest of her days dressed as a man,
hermit to the Mount of Olives,
beardless recluse forgotten by all;
of actresses, the patron saint.

THESE ERRORS ARE CORRECT (2008)

I wrote these poems for my wife
Shakti Bhatt
(1980–2007)

Praise for *These Errors Are Correct*

'In these poems, the theme of belonging is implicated in a variety of idiosyncratic ways: whether it's belonging to a drug ("the thick sweet amaze of heroin") or to a tribe empowered by metaphor ("it takes a lot / of cash to keep me / in the poverty to which I'm accustomed."); whether it's belonging to the hard-won zones between the local and the global, "between the spirit and the flesh" or to the spaces "between / thought and its correct / articulation" Thayil's poetry leaves the reader with a sense of danger, of language teetering wildly on the edge of some precipice, between centuries, between continents, between fleetingly improvised realms, suspended somewhere between history and invention, reality and nowhereness.'

Arundhathi Subramaniam, *Poetry International*

'Thayil's gift, coupled with a deep undercurrent of experience, makes it that rare book of poems where each one is worth going back to, time after time. One of India's most talented poets, Thayil experiments with ghazals, sonnets and the canzone to create a body of work that is haunting, distressing and beautiful; but not for the faint-hearted.'

Chinmayee Manjunath, *Elle*

'The poems in *These Errors Are Correct* are compressed, varied in mood and scene, but whether about history, religion, or some remembered disappointment, concern complexities of love and fate. There is also a surprising nostalgia for the pleasures and pains of drug addiction. Thayil compresses, occults, and his imagery is allusive and literary. He writes with a powerful voice and density of language and he make me think, even work, to understand his poetry. That he risks obscurity indicates how far Indian poetry in English has changed.'

Bruce King, *ReWriting India: Eight Writers*

Not Remembering

I lost the house. I lost the way home.
Not remembering is soulfood and music.
In 1975, I wrote a song that hit
the top of the Soul and Pop charts.
I was a One Hit Wonderbra.
Naranja estaba el colour de su vestido,
then silk blue. My wife died.
Many birds died. A bird readies the soul

and moves it to tenderness. I walked
from one end of town to the other.
A mezzo soprano sang arias
in my head. I gave away things.
Not remembering is a cathedral
where my hit song plays.

~

Democracy, the world's largest, arrived in our town the way
spring did, by throwing colour on the trees and on the faces
of strangers. Or maybe it was Socialism. (I'm not remembering
something each day.) Hello, meet your brother. He's not my
brother and neither are you. This was Old Delhi, soon after
the city was returned to us. To celebrate, we gave the streets
unpronounceable new names. So what if they were the names of
fools? At least they were our fools.

~

Beethoven loved cruelty as much as
he loved a cold water head bath. He says,

'I don't speak for the lily. War is an
expression of complex knowledge.' He den-

igrates dolphins and state funding for the
arts. He goes for days without an espress-

o.

Jesus said, 'Speaking is not my province.
You are.' He was speaking to his girlfriend.

Their words were encased in balloons but his
balloon was empty:

He changed his molecular linen. He
became oil based, a picture. The heart

wants to be attacked, the head to be crushed.

~

This is Bodhgaya where a leafless
tree gives more shade than
a house. To grow, all
you need is cruelty. The grand shade
trees expect to live to a respectable age.
Buddha said, 'Suffer
the parents.' Or maybe his editor

said that. I'm taking medication
to not remember. I
extricate myself for the violet
engine. I like the way the world
operates in the shade.
I promenade on the promenade and
suck my pill and fall

asleep. It wasn't that people
wanted a new life, they didn't
want the old one. Buddha said,

'Better to kill than to wound.'
I like that, I play it
loud in the car on my way to

Gandhi said Beethoven said Buddha said

~

Jesus proposed a new kind of writing, not
pictograms but broken lines. In Delhi we
invented aesthetic cleansing. We bused the
poor to quarters outside the city. Gandhi

was obsessed with bowel movements. 'Good morning,'
he said, 'did you have a good bowel movement
today?' We always replied. It was nearing
the mid-point of the century. What choice did

we have? The property dealers wanted a
share. They were men of vision. The head brims with
ideas when a crisis is near. Gandhi was
an example of algebraic notation.

Beethoven was obsessed with bowel movements.
Buddha was obsessed with bowel movements. But
Jesus was free of aesthetic cleansing. He
was without attributes. If you like, you can

take liberties with God, but with Mohammed
you must be watchful. The sick, the maimed, and the
talented are paraded each evening by
their families. They parade best if they've had

a drink, but not if they're drunk. The property
dealer's wife saw Jesus reading in the square.
She waited at his house with wine and fruit, but
he didn't open. Her husband went to see

her. 'Cruelty is only the first of many
options,' he said. 'There are other ways to change
your life.' She smiled but didn't speak. She wrote, 'I
know / there's little / chance of winning / his heart / but

I must try.' Her husband said, 'Mariana, I'm
rich, but my wealth no longer pleases me. My
loss doesn't bother me. Tell me what is wrong.'
She wrote, 'If you stand / against the light you will

see / that the spaces in your heart are clear, / all
except one. / This makes you mistake / the wisdom
of a sage / for a sickness.' 'I like your line
breaks,' said Jesus (through the door). 'But you should see

my girlfriend's.' (The heat was enormous, a blur of

~

My wife died. I
want to build a cathedral where birds
can worship. In Wy-
oming, working men were made to ride home
hungry if they didn't carouse
in the bars
after work. There's freedom and there's freedom.
They stare at you
if your eyes aren't blue. Jesus's eyes weren't blue.
It's easy to be Jesus
or Billy the Kid.
All you have to do is be cruel.
The Malabar Whistling Thrush anticipates our need
for applause.
His cry rambles up and down
the scale like a cell
phone tone
or sitcom laughter.

Beethoven suffered from the future.
Money was a consideration. Some worked like dogs
for it, some worked
against it. Once in a while, some jerk
made a paper boat.
Boggs
painted dollar bills.
He used them to pay for meals
in restaurants. Once, he received a painted repast.
He said, 'Fair exchange!' When a bird leaves the house
she lived in, she mourns, or she fasts
and sleeps, and builds in her sleep. Not
remembering
is a tall building, and a wedding ring.

Poem with Prediction

Because he's old and unsure,
he counts on your faith in images
and your fear, which is as pure
as when you were a child, turning the pages
of the illustrated books. He intones castrato *symbol* & basso *portent*,
reveals the unexpurgated blood truth of fairy tales, pretends
his closed, unchanged-in-2-millennia judgements
are improvised and no 5-star
disaster
awaits you. He gives you viral in exchange for Sister
Tree and calls it fair trade. You're allowed to whine
if you stay in key and watch your rhyme.
But your innocence
will be punished, this is a rule of the Great Gagadong.
Another is, You will love and obey him and let him lick
your wound with his infected tongue.
He brings you the good news—your tick
is erratic,
you are uninspired, dear
idiot, and no meaning will adhere
to you or your dead. His wide hand will rain
with blessings and good sense.
He'll translate the world into plain
language for you who are without ability. Your need for money
is as banal as it is weak.
The real work
is his to accomplish—in a week.
Your demands are too many,
your skin too soft. You deserve the paddle of his handmade violin.

Blue Ghazal

Give up your pen—you won't make a rhyme tonight.
The moon's cursed. Words are unsublime tonight.

Nobody's to blame, the note said nothing more.
I'm nobody; my love's not worth a dime tonight.

All's changed and the same across the black water.
Your mosambi is orange is sweet lime tonight.

Your killer smiles, offers Billie and a glass of wine.
I accept, she's my partner in crime tonight.

Fake it to make it, AA's coffee-drinkers intone.
No thanks, I'll take whisky and a white line tonight.

Self-loathing, thy proper name is poverty—
and poetry that wins no Guggenheim tonight.

A mystery to me: why are my friends so broke?
Call Mephisto, I'm ready for the big time tonight.

Broken moon, of broken blue and white china,
Only you are less hopeful than I'm tonight.

Jeet, why are you hungry when your bowl is full?
Are you sharing Shakti's paradigm tonight?

Premonition
for Shakti

1

Gone and *gone* doesn't mean a thing—
the world and we continue to be.
Happy to eat our pig and live, we sing
their names against the shame. We know
someone waits where the sky and sea
are tilted. She leans on light as on a floor.

The bridge between *is* and *was* descends
too soon, sweeps them up like chimney dust,
whose lips we loved, who were friends
when hands were hands that held us fast.
They reach to us, lost among the lost,
their shared minds stretched to the past,

inconsolable mouths slack with loss,
not able, not yet, to let go of us.

with a first line by Sebastian Mathews

2

In the hands of the priest
everything changed, even the feast

became ashes. He said, 'It's been long
enough that I've swung

around this high country's whipped winter
light, its bitter

water, the sick livestock,
the lack

of so much.' But in the sand-
stone city at noon, the sun's thousand

eyes looked for their king,
who was saying something.

The poor poured borrowed wine,
and practised for their big night of crying.

3

Sunday holds its head
in its hands, won't forget or shed

its unease, revisits the hard
word it spoke and heard

spoken, the secret unasked kiss.

At night, in my dream,
you return to ask the time,

and each time I make the same reply,
Better to die

than to lie like this,

without you.

Pale, already dressed
in his best,

Sunday speaks, but only about you.

4

Among the trees of the city,
full-throated Dracula Undulata

and Saddest, who shed in the first sun—
these were the trees he doted upon.

But the one he heard
all day, she was young, busy, bird-

full, her twiny, wing-bright head

like shining from shook foil,
her roots rowing deep in the soil.

Bend to him and give him food
from your lips. His mind is wood

and leaf, half buried in mud.
A touch will burst him to blood

and wake him, human on a bed.

5

To see if I'd still be here,
looking back at you, my figure
still, yours in motion, our
minds receding into the future,
the miles between us stretched like wire.
In my dream, it was a Sunday in summer
when you returned to the East River.
The city's last dogwood shivered
in the sun, but you didn't see her.
On the subway (your token had expired
years ago), you said, *Nothing's sadder
than this.* We found seats together.
I reached for you, but you weren't there.
Someone looked at me with pity and fear.

with a first line by Theresa Burns

To leave me on the F train, a lone
serenader
wailing Tom Waits circa *Bone
Machine* to the drunks and day traders

is not my idea of a hot first date.
The way you banged through the turnstiles
at Broadway and Lafayette
like you couldn't wait to put some miles

between your violincello
and my cherry red custom
Strat—well, what a show-stopping exit!
Enough to leave a fellow
with a life sized hole in his self esteem,
not to mention in his pocket.

with a first line by Elaine Sexton

7

to lick the meat from each other's bones
a star trembles in her long-gone burrow
she prepares, commits love marrow
gives the lie to the words *you fly, you fall*
neck black blood stones, her last tones
forever unspoken, one-sided, unequal

each dry mouthful the last
future sucked squirming to the past

a white room's bone white goodbye
its terrible news *no thing can stay*
nothing can stay a child's fall from a sky
the colour of old tragedy

two are twined in this sonnet
the bones got me started on it

with a first line by Ross Gay

8

To our bodies, expanding, numberless, slow,
August brought new knowledge of rain
gone berserk, of water pouring south.
Our dwarf palm stood with her mouth
open, making her objections plain,
dreaming, like us, of somewhere to go,

somewhere safe from the sea come to live
among us. But the streets were gone,
taken by a colour not-quite-green,
in which something unseen
waited to greet us. Even the sun
went under. It was time to leave,

but how could we outrun the weather?
Where could we go, and stay together?

with a first line by Elaine Sexton

9

    Forget the sea, let it fade.
How much longer can the craziness last?
    It'll stop
as soon as you imagine a new lost
    landscape
in which water and wind won't make a sound,
    Republic of the Not-Yet-Found,
a place you've seen before and where you've stayed.

    Only forget the town's old
name, the taste of apples, the words you know
    as your own.
Someone new is coming through; you should go,
    not home,
not backwards, but out where the light is wide
    and those you lost are by your side,
radiant, ambulant, their downed bodies whole.

Everybody forgets every dear thing.
I know how it goes. This is safe keeping.

with a first line by Curtis Bauer

10

When it rains, the dead descend, you appear,
the smell of rainwater in your hair,

wearing the ring I placed on your finger,
a scent like heat and a voice not yours, a
child's voice singing of age-old danger,
in Hindi, a lover's lament from *Pyaasa*.

Your lips, clear of the colour you wear,
are not new to me, are lovely and bare,

and our old argument still burns.
How soon will you forget me if I die?
By the river in this room and the way it returns,
I swear, If I forget you, let everything die.

When it rains the dead ascend, disappear
where we cannot follow, into the living air.

with a first line by Michelle Yasmin Valladares

Flowers for a Parijat

Being interested in travel
to places of disorder,
your gift was to unravel
distance, move between lovers,
understand each new border
as something always porous,
like the figures in your bed.
You were not to be trusted.
Only open to desire,
    to everyone,
      man and woman,
you were addicted to fire

and the sudden flame that flared
from each slight change in the wind.
What you loved most was the *where*,
a clear road, dry earth and sky,
space infinite in between.
And in that rush, who was I?
Designated ferryman,
loyal seeing-eye companion,
cool handler of your crashes
    and collected
    works, elected
the keeper of your ashes,

a role swiftly grown absurd
when I turned into your twin,
faithless as the broken word
spoken by my human tongue:
I'll be here to let you in.
But I was gone, out among
the pretty and the jaded,
the night I most was needed.
To carry now in my head

      blood images,
      black smeared pages
out of time, of you just dead,

ropes of blood around your neck,
blood flowers pressed to your face,
colour in your house turned black,
breath of lilies from your lips,
black with secrets, blood in place,
spears of blood sunk past their tips;
and I, nerves opened to god,
strain to hear his hideous word.
Like talent, the gift you left
    is fraught, a curse.
    Than this, no worse,
a phrase. I don't trust myself.

After

Your name is different there, it has no hook
    for sound,
and if sometimes you hear it called, a look
will show that no one spoke your name aloud,
or said anything at all, what you heard
    was just a recollected word.

The tables there are long enough to fit
    them all,
the many generations who will sit
together in their prime, will drink and tell
each other things they could not say before,
    when words slammed open like a door

and such occasions did not end without
    a scene.
And more has changed, the gaze that would report
your gaze is gone. You see the eyes you seem
to know, but you cannot remember how,
    or if it matters anymore.

for Philip Nikolayev

The Annotated Gita

Everything that lives, will live
    forever,
    will live whatever
    the odds they receive,
in rooms that resemble no rooms we know.

What if this time the small show
    were to pass?
    And if the sickness
    take off its pale blue
mask and apron, what then would we recall

of pain? It comes to us all.
    Everything
    that happens, happened
    already several
times before, will happen in the future.

That's unchanged. And now you're here
    you may as
    well try the windows
    and figure out where
they are, the rails of light you've seen out there.

To Baudelaire

I am over you at last, in Mexico City,
in a white space high above the street,
my hands steady, the walls unmoving.
It's warm here, and safe, and even in winter
the rain is benign. Some mornings I let
the sounds of the plaza—a fruit seller,
a boy acrobat, a woman selling
impossible fictions—pile up in a corner
of the room. I'm not saying I'm happy
but I am healthy and my money's my own.
Sometimes when I'm walking in the market
past the chickens and the pig smoke,
I think of you—your big talk and wolf's heart,
your Bonaparte hair and eyes of Poe.
I don't miss you. I don't miss you when
I open a window and light fills the room
like water pouring into a paper cup,
or when I hear a woman's white dress shine
like new coins and I know I could follow
my feet to the river and let my life go
away from me. At times like this,
if I catch myself talking to you,
I'm always surprised at the words I hear
of regret and dumb boyish devotion.

The Heroin Sestina

What was the point of it? The stoned
life, the chased, snorted, shot life. Some low
comedy with a cast of strangers. Time
squashed flat. The 1001 names of heroin
chewed like language. Nothing now to know
or remember but the dirty taste

of it, and the names: snuff, Death, a little taste,
H—pronounce it etch—, sugar, brownstone,
scag, the SHIT, ghoda gaadi, #4 china, You-Know,
garad, god, the gear, junk, monkey blow,
the law, the habit, material, cheez, heroin.
The point? It was the wasted time,

which comes back lovely sometimes,
a ghost sense say, say that hard ache taste
back in your throat, the warm heroin
drip, the hit, the rush, the whack, the stone.
You want it now, the way it lays you low,
flattens everything you know

to a thin white line. I'm saying, I know
the pull of it: the skull rings time
so beautiful, so low
you barely hear it. Itch this blind toad taste.
When you said, 'I mean it, we live like stones,'
you broke something in me only heroin

could fix. The thick sweet amaze of heroin,
helpless its love, its know-
ledge of the infinite. Why push the stone
back up the hill? Why not leave it with the time-
keep, asleep at the bar? Try a little taste
of something sweet that a sweet child will adore, low

in the hips where the aches all go. Allow
me in this one time and I'll give you heroin,
just a taste
to replace the useless stuff you know.
Some say it comes back, the time,
to punish you with the time you killed, leave you stone

sober, unknowing, the happiness chemical blown
from your system, unable to taste the word *heroin*
without wanting its stone one last time.

Malayalam's Ghazal

Listen! Someone's saying a prayer in Malayalam.
He says there's no word for 'despair' in Malayalam.

Sometimes at daybreak you sing a Gujarati garba.
At night you open your hair in Malayalam.

To understand symmetry, understand Kerala.
The longest palindrome is there, in *Malayalam*.

When you've been too long in the rooms of English,
Open your windows to the fresh air of Malayalam.

Visitors are welcome in The School of Lost Tongues.
Someone's endowed a high chair in Malayalam.

I greet you my ancestors, O scholars and linguists.
My father who recites Baudelaire in Malayalam.

Jeet, such drama with the scraps you know.
Write a couplet, if you dare, in Malayalam.

Spiritus Mundi

I was born in the Christian South
of a subcontinent mad for religion.
Warriors and zealots tried to rule it.
A minor disciple carried his doubt
like a torch to temple and shrine.
I longed for vision and couldn't tell it.

The cities I grew up in were landlocked.
One, a capital, buff with architecture,
the other lost for months in monsoon.
One was old, one poor; both were hot.
The heat vaporized thought and order,
drained the will, obliterated reason.

I settled, 20 and morose, in a town
built by a patricidal emperor
whose fratricidal son imprisoned him,
for eight years, with a view of the tomb
he built for his wife, to remember her.
I was over conscious of my rhyme,

and of the houses, three, inside my head.
In the streets, death, in saffron or green,
rode a cycle rickshaw slung
with megaphones. On the kitchen step
a chilli plant grew dusty in the wind.
In that climate nothing survived the sun

or a pickaxe, not even a stone dome
that withstood 400 years of voices
raised in prayer or argument. The train
pulled in each day at an empty platform
where a tea stall that served passers-
by became a famous fire shrine.

I made a change: I travelled west
in time to see a century end
and begin. I don't recall the summer
of 2001. Did it exist?
There would have been sun and rain.
I was there, I don't remember

a time before autumn of that year.
Now 45, my hair gone sparse,
I'm a poet of small buildings:
the brownstone, the townhouse, the cold water
walkup, the tenement of two or three floors.
I cherish the short ones still standing.

I recognize each cornice and sill,
the sky's familiar cast, the window
I spend my day walking to and from,
as if I were a baffled Mughal in his cell.
I call the days by their Hindu
names and myself by my Christian one.

The Atlantic's stately breakers mine
the shore for kelp, mussels, bits of glass.
They move in measured iambs, tidy
as the towns that rise from sign to neon sign.
Night rubs its feet. A mouse deer starts across
the grass. The sky drains to a distant eddy.

Badshah, I say to no one there.
I hear a koel in the call of a barn owl.
All things combine and recombine,
the sky streams in ribbons of colour.
I'm my father and my son grown old.
Everything that lives, lives on.

Letter from a Mughal Emperor, 2006

Nothing here's worth a tick.

I hid everything except the heads. They respect slaughter.

They respect only slaughter. They forget the other things we brought them, the ghazals, the gardens, the ice and symmetry.

It's an affliction to grow up motherless, with your lady mother living beside you.

They have many images, but they have no God. They're fit only for war.

Even the dogs are second rate.

In Tashkent I had no money, no country or hope of one, only humiliation. But among the people I found much beauty. No pears are better.

There are no accidents. There's only God.

Tending to his doves on the eve of battle, my father flew into a ravine at the fortress of Akhsi.

He became a falcon. I became emperor.

Sometimes, when I eat a Kabul melon, I remember my father and you.

I've forgotten more than I've seen, but I haven't forgotten enough.

There's only one way to live in a place like this, with your disgust close at hand.

One night I took majoun because the moon was shining. The next day I took some more, at sunrise.

I enjoyed wonderful fields of flowers, flowers on all sides. I saw an apple sapling with five or six leaves placed regularly on each branch.

No painter could have done this.

I made a schedule. Saturday, Sunday, Tuesday and Wednesday for wine, the other days for majoun.

Your letter puzzled me:

The people are caught between constant spiritual anguish and a faith that will give meaning to the question that consumes them: the dual substance of Krishna, the yearning of man to know God. Between the spirit and the flesh, a great unwinnable war.

Dear friend, write clearly, with plain words. Writing badly will make you ill.

Once, in an orchard, I was sick with fever and vision. I was young, but I prepared myself.

A hundred years or a day, in the end you'll leave this place.

Long ago, my grandfather's face looked into mine, I think with love.

Now when we speak it's of ghazals, of metrics and rhyme or of our most famous massacres.

When he conquered Lahore he planted a banana tree. It thrived, even in that climate.

His memory is so good it gives him a second life. Mine gives only a partial one.

It's no more than I need.

The Two Thousands

In the end it took so little to do us in:
the imaginative use of fuel,
the fuzzy grammar
of this or that group of logicians,
gifts of money
to the strongest among us.
Who could resist those voices raised in unison?
'Travel broadens nothing,'
the Great Martyr said, 'except your tan.'
It was the official position,
broadcast without commercial interruption
every evening at 6.
The time for lyricism had passed.
Also—kissing, sculpture, coq au vin, the tango,
and other items of behaviour
too commonplace to mention.
They had G_D on their side;
we had fear.
Same difference, you might have said.
I kept a wet finger to the wind.
Depending on who was winning
I shaved or I didn't.

A History of Religion

Annie chops her notebook
into unequal pieces. I sneak a look

at the words that appear
on her page, 'I'm alone here.'

You are
alone, and distant as a star

without a name. Alone myself,
lost in a hieroglyph,

I measure the rain that blurs
our house,

the infinite, the enormous rain,
unstoppable in its broken

run to the sea.
But I keep my ears peeled,
and my eyes, Annie,

for red flash, or squeal
of rubber,
for any sign of Time's arrival

in our border
town;
or a man, a pious body robber

whose eyes sink like the sun
in your sweet, dangerous, open

face.
If I watch for the tide to rise

and break,
we'll be fine. If I stay awake.

Cut to Bits by the Sickle Moon

Who has done this?
Schoolboys, drained of
all emotion but the one
that'll outlast them,
kneeling on the sands in
waves through the two
thousands, learning the
fundaments of blood
sacrifice as the correct
response to figurative art.

Why Should You Believe Me?

How can we be sure he was among us,
when the signs speak only of his absence,
the garden denuded, stones washed clean
of blood, the story ended as if he'd never been?
Djinn, angel, sweet enemy, help me make sense
of the life we led and the kiss that stung us.

You forgot too much. You were dazzled, in thrall
to his beauty, his recall—bored, casual,

perfect—of the future. You knew nothing else,
except you were lost with and without him.
Luck of some kind brought us to the Arameans,
whose great disappointment was that pain
purified us. When they ask me about him
I say, he was my king and he was false.

with a first line by Julia Cole

The Origin of Remorse

It wasn't rain, but giant
wings that encircled
them with sound. When
one walked forward
to check the contours
of the land, the sharp,
the blood-sharp
feathers drove
him back to the rock
where his friends waited
with the rags and bits
of paper they held
up for protection.
They stumbled forward,
blind, and thought
of turning back
and knew they could not,
that the open unlit
plain was better
than the rude welcome
waiting at home.
Sometimes, someone
fought to stand
and speak, but the sky
forced him down
until his will dissolved
and he broke to the ground.

Wagah

I should have ducked
when I saw the warning flare
hit the flatbed
Tata
supply truck
and the *Horn. OK. Please Keep
Distance* sign lit up an improbable red.
But I didn't dare
interrupt
the baby's sleep
and besides, I knew
hostilities would erupt
when the senior dancer
dropped her
veil. Imagine my surprise when this shrew,
this milk-white matron burst
into a medley
of Lata
Mangeshkar hits,
and the rival generals,
dewy-
eyed, ordered sherbets
from Nirula's
and embraced.

War is Work

Whatever it's about it's not about
this, this
sitting around shooting
the bull with your best buddy, your fat
ass parked on my time.
Listen, hoss/dawg/hombre/homie,
it don't matter to me if you're drinking
Bud on the roof with your shirt
gone, smiling at the Gorgons and their mossy
cheeks, or praying
to the pigeons, you know,
confessing your misery, or bowing
from the hips to the river.
I'm cool, I'm down-
town with that,
and I'm no kind of stickler for logic neither,
which, ha
ha,
you know. I don't believe
in your abundance of reason,
your 1 love, 1 world, 1 life, 4 wives,
your unity of all
faiths—
I mean, what's that mean?
Here's what I know,
I know from a) bringing it on
and b) getting it done
and c) knowing who my friends are.
You know who your friend is?
Yeah, no!
You see night
security tell him to stop with the cook
fires in the backyard, I can't use
the extra business. We got to keep it

real down
here, with our boys away
plugging the dam.

View from the Ground

Never easy, the way the body falls
into its web of blood
each morning, and you rise
like someone waiting to be consoled.

The truth arrives too late
to change the facts.
This is you
and this is your view—
dawn, a smashed street,
the hospital cart rolling past.

The woman won't move just yet.
She marks the exact spot
with her eyes, and waits and waits
to open the door and walk to it.

Two Interventions

They bar us from the republic
because we do what they cannot.
We combine spirit conjecture
and a description of the sea,
say the North Sea at 5 a.m.

In July, the city returns to the desert.
A man dresses his wife in a sheet
the colour of mourning. She walks to
market for his breakfast meat.
He watches the TV news. His job
is to sing, five times daily,
the amplified hymns of truth.

Nativism

At 48, the youngest
director in the history of the Civil
Center for Falconry,
Universal Understanding & Aesthetic
Interest,
he published *The Spiritual Uses of Oneiric
Travel*. It was wartime,
but there's little trace of conflict
in this odd and beautiful collection
of travel jottings, doodles, and rhyme.
'Everywhere in the old city
there was dread,
a sense of ancient
sympathy,
of inebriated spirits taking the dead,
imperial government
to task, while its citizenry
and civil
servants slept.'
In subsequent decades, he refined his view
of history as the art of the impassable.
He wrote that his goal had been
to be wholly adept
at transference, 'a bridge between
thought and its correct
articulation.'
When the government fell he lost his new
stipend, a palpable
loss, and he went home to die.
It was his last
act of secular defiance.
Varanasi, inauspicious
in the new theology, was a dry
tiered place of souls
whose chance on earth had passed,

who concerned themselves
with 'a wider world, a suspicious
heritage,
a secure context for the cosmic dance,
a swift descent, a dangerous old age.'

Superpower

Leap tall buildings in a single bound? Forget
you, buddy, I
leap years, avenues,
financial/fashion/meatpacking districts, 23
MTA buses parked end to
end. I leap Broadway,
yoyo to
traffic light, to
bus top, to Chrysler, to jet.
You need a mind of sky, of rubber,
to understand I. You need
silence, cunning. Exhale!
You need to know that everything is metaphor,
that poems sprout
in my hands
like mystic confetti, like
neural string theory.
My brother, Mycroft, is tiny, but a genius,
oh a tiny genius, whose
'art is subtle, a precision of hallucinatory brilliance,'
—that's serious talk, boy—
he's 'furthermore' and 'however,' I'm
'know what I'm saying?' and 'whatever.'
He is the ghost ant, the one who is not
there, unseen until he stops
moving. I am
companion to owl and peregrine,
emperor of air, and I'm loyal
to you my loyal subject, whose hard-won
pleasure I perform,
and though I'm not rich it takes a lot
of cash to keep me
in the poverty to which I'm accustomed.

The Sonneteer

I was famous, I won the Hawthornden prize.
Girls flashed me. One said, 'You're the poet, right?
What a godawful waste it would be, otherwise.'
I told her my talents would not last the night,
and it *was* a waste, you bet, any which way.
She said, 'Poetry boy, I don't give a damn.
I've got time to kill, make a sonnet for moi.'
'She hawks her beauty in the night,' I began,
and stopped, unable to motor my mouth.
One morning I stepped out for cigarettes
and hopped a subway to the south—
I thought I'd vanish myself and my debts.
For months she heard my step on the stair.
It wasn't me, brothers, I was taking the air.

The Parrot of Happiness

I buried the snowshoes.
Buried the training wings and folding cot,
the book of easy-to-learn Braille curses.
Your parrot kicked up a riot.

He clicked the afternoon's fine
weaves one colour at a time.

Colours like a delicatessen.
No room for delight or precision,

just big opinions droned
for hours, in a rude baritone.

Now I'm sinking boilermakers
and I won't stop. I'll come to with a wife,
in Buenos Aires,
thinking of maps, my blindness, the good life.

The Miniature

Her wheatish complexion lit by the sun,
    a woman leans
into latticed stonework and breathes, summoned
by her husband who wants her to watch him,
    watch from behind the screens
as he decides a man's life. They will dim

in time, their outlines form a rough zero,
    bits of inlay
will be missing, a future made clearer,
and a restorer will work his slow art,
    but no labour will stay
the change to come, or her quickening heart.

Against Gravity

Objects in that room reflected nothing
    but light, where
    it seemed as if each bright thing,
    the mirror, the floor, the chair,
    was something
other than itself, something high like air,

and it seemed as if we too would outpace
    the present,
    would make our story weightless,
    unchanging, a firmament
    and a space
that told us what was there was permanent.

Dear Heptanesia,

When you stop on Market Street
for more anaesthesia,
pick up some supplies
—brandy, papayas,
The Marsh Province Buys,
and oil
for the kerosene lamps.
Or else how will
the mail boat find us when
the power fails,
as it so often
does in these wretched swamps?
I need a hose, 7-gallon pails
(the frangipani's
drowning in the heat),
a large black brolly,
and 2 DVDs: *Pennies
from Heaven* and *Pope Pius:
His Story.* When you return, I'll be up
waiting, not tired.
I like it that you're here
helping me cope.
I like to know you're in the room,
a little out of range,
not saying anything
but letting me know I'm not alone,
not entirely.

The New Island

Once, carried by the rains of September,
a boat lifted free of its mooring place,
of a shed become part of the river,
    and floated past
      the porch, where I caught her.

Somehow the house kept itself clear of the
river that had made it a new island,
but everything around us was water.
    I made the stern
      seesaw with every step.

You were lining up the prow with a tree
I thought too far upstream in the blurred tides
of current to be trusted. Now I'm sorry
    I held the sides
      as we climbed the water.

Your hands, as you moved us forward, were sure
in their shaping of water, your eye true,
and our few feet of hammered wood, our floor,
    took us in to
      lamplight, voices, the shore.

Aquatic

Who will speak to the fish in their shiver?
They've heard it before,
your lie, that a river runs under the river.

Movement is bliss, a kiss their claim.
They visit your room
and stay up nights to dream,

on their side of the glass,
entranced by your colour in the kitchen lights.
They hang, breathing with their mouths,

speaking of the gorgeous life, the glisten.
Suspended in the supreme element,

they murmur your name as the days
turn warmer, colder, stranger, your 1,000 names

recited in pairs,
follow one on one like stairs

to the high surface of the water,
where it's hot, or it's hotter,

where everything floats and smells,
and you'll need a new set of skills—
vigilance, silence, gills.

Verticality

Start with fish.
Add multiple legs and the word *night*.
Add a pair of legs, upright, and a pair of lungs.
Add the sound of (violent) mastication.

~

The sky is familiar. Add the passing of time.

~

Served to the servant, good coffee in a tiny cup.
Once we were the same, we were not divided by name.
Add red.

~

That year the truffles were plentiful. We were outdoors all day.
The Signora instructed us in packing and preparation.

Water splashing in a stone basin, the hurried walk across the piazza. And later her voice, *Nel cieco mondo*. And mine, *Who is blinder than I am now?*

Now is the present where this story is told, *there* is the world of the dead.

Add a place where nothing shines.

~

The Canto that begins with hoar frost and ends, abruptly, with
   fish scales on a dry branch.
The Canto that sits on the same descending axis as Jerusalem.
The Canto of *begat* that lists names in sequence, lineage and
   marital ties intact on page after page of beautiful type, very
   small, to be whispered like a prayer for protection.
The Cantor's Canto.
The Canto found in an earthen pot in a field in Upper Egypt.

The Canto in which nothing adds up.
The Canto that propels the eye off the page.
The terrible Canto we cannot repeat for fear.
A cantilever.
The Canto recited on the battlefield.
The Canto of surrender in the forest to the boy with the dark blue skin.
The Canto of Renunciation.
The missing Canto.
The Canto of Dis.
The Canto that hides a fatwa in its first letters.
The Canto with the uncut pages.
The Canto with a watermark so elaborate it is invisible to the human eye.
The Canto with no friends except a bottle of smashed green.
The Canto Maudit.
The Canto en plein air, ou je ne comprends rien.
The Canto the Chairman knows by heart.
The Canto that will go off for a decade of severe self-criticism.
The Canto that rides in on a saddle of meat, long beard greasy, eager to meet your tallest buildings.
The Wall Street Canto datelined the day after tomorrow.
The Canto Leaves Home Early and Finds Slaughter in the Street.

~

The inner courtyard was submerged, everywhere the smell of burning. Each step a wading in honey and we no closer to the whetstone porch. My eyes were on the cistern, where a crown of wolf bees worked in silence. The night burned its red candles. Inside, she held her hands open like a book. She offered the layered marks on her neck as continuing proof of her love.

~

'blotched with reddish brown' occurs frequently in *The Book of Hyphenated Birds (Vol. VII, Asian-American).*

E.g.: ...*tree or cornice or roof of a building. Eggs, 2 to 4, dirty pinkish white, lightly spotted and blotched with reddish brown.*

And: *...in the fork of a large banyan or similar tree, varying from white to pale brick red, blotched with reddish brown or blackish, heavily at the broad end; very handsome.*

And: *They scrape in the ground lined with grass*
     brood and rear at the edge of a swamp
     preferably near streams or clearings
     with grass forming a bower-like arch
     creamy buff or pale salmon or handsomely matt
     prodigiously blotched with reddish brown
     eggs laid on bare ground in bamboo or bush
     as many as 13 in a cup-shaped depression.

~

Nikolay, where is beauty? *It is in the wine that loves us.*

And God? *In the bread which is in the oven.*

Where is sorrow? *In each mouthful of air.*

And beauty? *In the woman whose lot it is to wear us down then delight us.*

~

Add: here's everywhere.

~

the inconveniences that have happened to some
persons which have transported themselves from England
to *Virginia*, without provisions necessary
to sustain themselves, has greatly hindered the progress
     of that noble plantation
     for prevention of the like
     disorders hereafter, that
     no man suffer, either through

ignorance or misinformation, it is thought
requisite to publish this short declaration
wherein is contained a particular of such like
necessaries, as either private families or
    single persons shall have cause
    to furnish themselves with, for
    their better support at their
    first landing in *Virginia;*

whoever transports himself or any
woman at his own charge to *Virginia*
    shall for each person so
    transported before
    Midsummer of this year
    have to him and his heirs

fifty acres of land upon a hill.

~

The trees had no colour. They smelled of fear.

You heard the sea's steady beat.
You heard time hiss on the tarmac. It said one word, *Gone.*

Your thoughts turned phosphorescent, appeared and disappeared
like pineapple fish.

You were made up of points of light, each point a mind.
You could not go dark.

Dietary Habits in the Mountains

The yak is allowed because one sustains many.

Fish are not, it takes too many to feed a man.

No root vegetables, many systems depend on them.

Humans are allowed, especially if they're vegetarian.

The Cook's Tale

Always born in some close
body, its questionable colour,
marigold ending & practice of loss,

memorizing the lessons of tequila
to compose our psalms in code.
2C & a Sea. To go, double carajilla.

To serve the Great Food
Court of America
& its true horizon, a line of blood,

the body awake, automatic, a
groove of chop & knead
in last night's stained tunic, a

paper cap tilted
down, brain & nose fused
like arithmetic to the wide

instant in the first
touch of oil. When Hector says, 'Half land,
half sea,' the room accelerates past

each working fire-lit hand,
& by the tendon's flare & cramp
we see how meat will end.

The world too: by fire. Whose crimped
hair, whose flashing headband
leads us? Appearing in the lamp-

light of his arms, our captain's,
whose figure we follow, whose fall,
if it comes, will mean the end

of a city's unwriteable style.
The one who leads doesn't look back.
To turn is to let the future fall

backwards into a dark
where no hope is,
to dishonour the years of smack

& rehab, the 12 tasks he set himself.
But they wait for Hector's
attention, our chief

parishioners, our co-actors,
each a partner & friend
in the legend of Flaming Embers,

waiting for Hector to say when
to step up for their reward,
Hector, whose epic invention

lines the grill in charred,
flame-braised intervals, who's
saying, 'Speak, I ain't heard

you, man,' his plate-sized
T-bones made to order,
secret salsa,

El Rio del Perdido,
& *Nuyorican Sour Cream*,
Hector,

who speed-fills a tray in real time
& slows it to you,
inert like someone in a dream,

your hands outstretched, your two

eyes wide, your mouth open
as you receive the food,

exhausted by the current
that ties you to him, to his
brilliant, bored, forgiving

hands. You, there among the chairs
—where the poor surrender—
are the sole source

of light in a crowded room, your
senses alert,
your steps halt with tender-

ness, your food hot.
At 3 p.m. when you're gone,
Hector will prepare a take-out

bag with his own vegetarian
meal. He'll pack
away his headband & apron,

& walk
like an ordinary man
to the park.

My Lie

If you marry me
I'll give you this poem
in which a ship full of men,
hoarse from drinking,
pull themselves through a sea
boiling with rain.
It's an epic poem
on which I've been
working
so long my eyes have dimmed.
It's yours if you marry me.

My Paris

Maybe in the slow, reptilian Seine,
where my friend, Paul Ancel,
tries tonight to recombine
his sweet, anagrammatic cells.
Or on a bridge, or on the banks,
with folded hands, giving thanks.

Maybe with a half baguette
and my one coffee of the day,
or sipping on a cigarette,
self-rolled, in the Greek café.
At sunset, maybe, in the Tuileries,
speaking to my sweeties the trees.

Or on a bench in the sun
in the Rue Boucherie, kicking it
with Our Lady of the Stone
Face and Troubled Spirit.
Maybe asleep in the bookshop,
maybe waiting for the rain to stop.

Maybe on the Metro, singing
my three and a half songs—
'Visions of Johanna,' 'Smokestack Lightning,'
and a medley, 'Hallelujah/Tower of Song'—
carried by *the major lift, the minor fall*
to the seven stations of the busker's mile.

Nowhere near the Eiffel Tower,
not unless I've lost my way.
Not at the Pompidou Center
or walking on the Champs Elysees.
Not even in the Louvre,
gawking at the Mona Lisa.

Migration

The cripple and his Inner Riches,
pictured in the near windows
of aspectless houses, of TV noise

and a child's repeated 'I don't want.'
Evening hovers above the strand
like caught exhaust that won't descend

or lift, intoxicated hue of burst
orange, the bloom blown. Slowing past
houses and a house, and it's

not that he wants a place
at their table, but a moment to rest,
watch a head speak human news,

discuss some small unimportant,
his voice lowered, his gaze distant,
the drink cold in his hand, ice melted

like bubbles of the mermaid's saying,
her rising call, 'Jake, is that you?'
And he's 10 years gone and the same,

still unsure, revising the air, the frost,
the penguins arcing like his best thoughts.

Gabreel in America

Strips of rain, white
sheets cut and knotted.
The moon's half-sister
eels to heel, elongated,
a new river
on 87th Street.

A plane tree shifts
years, gathers close
her daughters.
On the walk, bareheaded,
a man slows his slender
face. Open at the window,
I search the sky. There.
No, there.

My brothers are late, so late
they won't know me. I have changed.
I've aged 70
years or weeks. In this city
or another.

We were one, once, before I came here.

Late Vespers at the Hudson

1. UNTITLED

Poem of no cleverness—
no list of bird names,
just one bird awake in the moonlight.
No colour, no sound,
just this street at 4 a.m.

Not high, or drunk on language.
Saying one small thing
to a broken beat,
homemade like this poem.

Poem like my son
whom I have never seen
and hope I never will.

And you who I won't meet again but in dreams.

Poem to welcome myself home,
without honour or ease.
With this drink,
my first in five years,
I open my arms to you.

2. A CURE

You can beg all you want,
it won't do a thing.
Dr Dilaudid's withholding your privileges.

Across the hall your friend
with the black eye
is telling his visitors you are insane,
which you are.

He smokes unfiltered cigarettes.
When he isn't smoking he's eating.
One night he stood in your room
reciting obscenities
until the words peeled away
from their meanings.

Your walk will be cancelled today.
You will eat alone.

The woman who sits
most mornings by your bed
will leave early.

Too distracted to speak,
you watch a small flesh-coloured spider
levitate with happiness in the window.

3. SUBLINGUAL

Miracle—no other word for it—
pill that transforms

a monkey into a man.

No word except *methadone*,
that I placed under my tongue

each day for three years
until he disappeared,

leaving a taste like ash
on the lips of a dead friend.

4. RECOVERY, PARTIAL

On the third month
of my forty-fourth year,
I wake on the southwest corner
of 87th street.

I have a scar on my belly,
old punctures on my arms,
a bad liver.
I have problems sleeping.

But I know I can wake
without hearing the old command,
'Feed me or else.'

I am fearful this gift will pass
and take with it everything,
my new life in a city of fragile buildings,
small needs for bread or coffee
or a shared cigarette,
the smoke flattened by rain.

5. STEP EIGHT

How can I make amends to you
who are beyond reach?

What use are words that arrive
in silence?

I am bringing you a list,
20 years long,

of unforgivable things I have done,

my only achievement a long,
reasoned derangement,

and this apology made too late.

I want you to know that I
am having dinner with friends.
They are drinking whisky and wine.

I'm drinking coffee, and I am fine.

6. UNTITLED

A long time ago or this morning,
I saw your face and knew time
for what it was—a coil
stretched both ways at once,
infinite and negotiable.

I'm walking now in April snow
without hope of finding you,
knowing you are gone
like a street closing under water.

I'm feeding coins into a payphone,
trying to hold on to your voice,
*Why did you change so much,
what happened to the man I knew?*

He's still around, somewhere close,
watching me work
my paranoia, my ailment,
my lovingly crafted ransom note.

7. UNTITLED

Asp I took into my vein,
whose bite appeared 20 years later.

Is that you?
Or the 87th Street bird returned
from a night on the town,

as we sit here silent,
my silent wife and I
who wonder at your thirst.

8. LATE VESPERS AT THE HUDSON

From those to whom much is given
much will be taken away.

I ask for nothing more.

I am standing with my head down.
If you want, I'll stand here all night
in the wind come raw from the river.

My tree is the weeping cedar.
My only verb 'to wait'.

I am ragged with staring for you.

In the City of Insomnia

There's a parade in the white
streets of the city. All night

the armoured cars trundle past
the avenue. Dazed

men and women stand,
making circles with their hands,

their smudged
eyes wide

open. At dawn the silent mayor
arrives, climbs the stairs

to your room, takes a moment
to catch his breath and presents

you with a key you will wear
round your neck like a star.

Grand Central, 2003

Still time for the grief, the note and its revelation years into the future.

I'm sorry

No one's to blame

The 8.05 White Plains local. You, wrapped in something heavy, an orange spot in a sea of spots marching with your brothers into the great cathedral, *un*lost, pulled forward on a beam of new light that comes from every direction at once, your veins brimming, afloat in the infinite filament where a bright head lifts star-filled hands spread to bless, on the day of your first communion.

I'd leave you there but abandonment is not an option, not this time, with the indicator ticking through its sermons and the ground level apse ready for the midnight season. How will you move without my voice in your ear? Who will show you to the Lost & Found, through the bad hours until sunrise when the lower lobby armchairs are available once again for your contemplations?

You are Here

The bees of summer sail the avenues
like lovers. It's June but cool, and the news

isn't new: no change in your fortune,
not in the proximate future,

not for the better. You talk of cities
you won't see again. One, to the East,

is pounded by rain for half the year,
for the other half it stews in fear

of its own dialects. Its Victorian stations,
water stained, are eye-catching ruins,

like the six-legged monuments
to British adulterers. Sex and violence,

casual as the monitor licking lunch from the air,
scraps the estranged mind will share.

Led by One Law for Aliens and your own lack

of foresight, you do a dance: two steps back,

best foot forward. A future races the street,
draws even with the corner, you in pursuit,

following like another Orpheus,
his three friends still friends, his voice

intact, no plans for a moonlit headlong swim,
his wife at the window waiting for him.

Flight

How did we know to go, to obey?
How did we come to be refugees,

our household scattered, an eastward breeze
our guide? We were ghosts, not from the past

but from a future that would last
no longer than a season.

We hoped to be led by a star or by reason,
but were taken by circumstance, by its

furious, arbitrary dance, like poets
of a line defined by rhyme,

our stanzas shaped by chance and time.
The slanted lines and inverted minarets

of Arabic, on successive jets,
took us 8,000 miles from the city,

from the impossibility
of our lives. We were headed

home, but home wasn't where we'd left it.
Here, nothing moves but wilts. The banyan

digs its fingers in for rain,
and finds the sun. Bird cries fill the sky.

Of them all, the koel it is whose song I
hear all night long, a coagulating widow's

song that clogs the windows
and the ears. Like the unreliable,

the inconsolable koel
who makes her home where she finds it,

I make my home with you, in transit.
The continent drops away and reappears,

its slow, ash-choked rivers rehearse
a brilliant future from a time long gone,

and the koel rehearses her song,
You and you are here to stay.

The Penitent

I'm back where my life and I parted ways.
I'm talking to the coffeemaker, to the face
towels folded by the sink, to the air
conditioner that conspires with my enemies. Even now,
in the midst of my extremity, my eyes are dry,
and if I jump repeatedly against the window
I can tell myself I'm being lifted by a great joy—
until the glass smites my face and I cry out
your old name. The room is empty, lonely
as a still life, but the water stains speak
with your voice, *Honour me, honour everything.*

Quiet and Concerned with Provenance

Around the room, the names I did not know
grew into their faces like the flies.
The names, the faces grew like the flies, so
I grew too. Buzz was my new sound. My eyes

magnified, scraped to insomnia glass,
I went to the pitiless father and son
who froze the water into place,
whose boredom melted it down.

I'm asking, I said, for a little time.
I'll pay what I owe, just let me stay
a moment in the sun, correct my rhyme,
collect my mind, and take my leave of the day.

It struck me then I wouldn't speak again,
no one would, except the endless rain.

Big Yellow Music, Like

I like you in your new, whitewashed houses
whose front doors open on other houses,
where a night light burns like blood in a pool,
    your blood, used for firewood
to light the open road to the river.

Cool water, white water, receive this man
who walked across the city to slaughter,
walked as if he were only your daughter,
    and waited for a sound
remembered from before, and for the moon.

Brilliant and famous, my pale, pretend friend.
Everything works out (she says) in the end,
one or the other way. She sails her cave,
    its new edge newly frayed,
and I crawl from the field for my hunger.

Should I go, or continue to wait here?
Sometimes I hear the big yellow music
of hyacinths thudding when you speak.
    I'm sick of the future,
of bedtime stories from a page gone blank.

Without hope, without fear, by the river
and the moon, the soon-to-be-born arrive,
crowding the banks to see how I praise you.
    There's much they wish to know,
I show them my life of beautiful water.

The Eye

Five floors above the traffic of Bombay
a man settles down to his only choice
    of the day,
    a vapour trail of powder
so fine he could use it for fuel, or chase
it through a short valley in Idaho.

There's a ghost ship held hostage on the rocks
nearby. The sea or something greater than
    the sea locks
    the view in place, the morning
calm as a postcard, except for the man.
And we're there why? Not to stare but to bring

some context to the scene. We're there to say,
Hey Ram, what a tragic waste of a life,
    and to say,
    There but for the grace go I,
and to come home to our aperitif,
our kids in the bank, our all-seeing eye.

The Opposite of Nostalgia

I'm trying to forget
those days one day at
a time—
the pitiful rooms
with their puddles of light,
the women I haggled with,
the car stopped in the street,
the wife barefoot,
on the run,
car keys in her hand.
Or I'm there, the sum
of my ambition
defined by old
rage, my anger like a slow child
hitting out at anyone
who comes
her way. I'm thinking
of the negotiation
with strangers, the attempt to say
things differently,
the men's room at the airport,
the glassine bag, the rolled-up note,
the line hitting the back of my throat
with a kick
like an anesthetic,
and, later, the paramedic
saying I'm lucky
to be
alive, and telling him
he's wrong, I'm
not lucky or alive,
just high.

New Year, Goa

The midnight's cataracts whiten,
and here's the sea hissing
its one stuttered consonant.

Leaf-printed, you track the moon
to a beached, bearded hull, a room
of vertigo or freedom

that narrows like memory.
Small flames ascend a tree
of light. The two-and-thirty

palaces of Bodhisattvam
tremble on the vellum-
smooth water, like flotsam.

If tonight the mind is queasy,
drawing thoughts like flies, he
is fine too with every crazy

scheme you devise, none crazier
than this pilgrimage to a pier
that seems to have disappeared,

leaving you seaborne at last,
ahead of you the past,
and all its famous cities lost.

On Taking a Line for a Walk

Among the categories of disorder
    this one is supreme,
    the porous border
    between
    love and its cool exacting twin.

It's a word, yes, and something less, a real
    strip of hard median
    that says, 'Be not cruel,'
    the sign
    faded, consigned to oblivion.

After Brodsky

Here I am for a second Christmas,
by the banks, unfrozen, of the old Pontus.
At this longitude, the Star of Kings falls
directly above a flat horizon of harbour walls.
I wish I could say that I can't live
without you, but, as these lines prove,
I can. I've been wandering around. Here,
I trespass on the grass and down my beer.

I came south for the winter
and took my seat at our old café,
the Yalta, from where you and I
were catapulted into the future,
in proof of the law that no happiness
can last. With a finger, I draw your face
on poor man's marble, while nymphs
in heels give the room a glimpse

of skin. Tell me, you gods of the stained glass,
what were you trying to tell us?
All I see through the smeared window
is a dull point of light. Is that you?
Lines on the sea, my face: the future's arrived,
it tells us that after all we've survived.
Everything disappears, even the fiddler
will stop and take his music elsewhere.

Soon the sea, which isn't black at all, will crash
open the door and flood the rooms
where you drank wine and napped the afternoons
away, where you let the sun dry your blouse.
The sea, not we, will swamp the terrace,
the birch grove, our favourite walks, each place
we loved. It will flood the halls, silence the bells,
and make a home for molluscs and oyster shells.

The Art of Seduction

When the flooding in the basement got worse
she slipped into a silly dress

and danced to *The Best of Nirvana*.
The way she fell on the divan, her

arms open—*The best thing for stress*—

you could have been some guy brought home
to read *Confessions of an English Opium*

Eater louder over Kurt's guitars,

some guy who would spend the evening
cross-legged on a tatami mat,

listening for the words between the words.

Youth is wasted on the young
and wisdom on the old, you know that,

like the call of a rare, flightless bird.

Sonnets for the Mouth

1

Everything, everyone goes into that mouth.
You in that mouth, washed blue TV light,
tunnel light, cold hotel air,
food half eaten on a tray, someone there
on the carpet, sleeping maybe or tripping,
someone's cigarette saying, the way you open
your mouth like it's what, like satire but.
The slide, the pull, the come, the remark unfinished.
The pull come slides the unfinished remark
like it's open, like satire in your mouth.
The way your cigarette says someone, someone's
sleeping carpet maybe, half eaten on a tray.
Washed blue tunnel light, cold TV hotel,
you in that mouth eating everything.

2

Tongued smoke hanging stiff off the leather,
humid backseat slither, friction body hiss,
the guy pulled, in a frenzy, hard
pulse violet in the dashboard light,
stray information from some knowable source,
slick primal ambient drip,
the sound of suck when he sticks
his fingers inside you, & the man driving,
smoke tongue, friction hiss, all body,
slither pulse in the dashboard light,
the information inside you stuck,
humid leather violet from your stick,
your knowable primal ambient sound—
the man says excuse me and drips.

3

Your skin pulls air off the towers.
Humid body cut empty of light,
you're not coming but laughing.
The small marigold temple you live,
sky the colour of wedding rings,
old colour without salt or sound,
sand drift streets empty of leather.
Someone pulls you into scaffolding,
your skin grows small cuts cut slow,
old marigold without exit, stuck,
high pigment, high streets,
sunblock hard & empty of suck,
your tongued finger, dashboard pulse,
you on empty, ready to please.

4

Or adrift on a street, leaning into green,
checking drivers, willing to please.
Your skin pulls air off the towers,
slows down traffic, the breathing trees.
Lift up your top if that's what he wants,
open whatever, take cash then kiss.
The trees pull skin like scaffolding,
take it over you in a dirty scald,
a live marigold show for the small sky.
Adjust yourself as you leave his car,
colour of rings & icons,
say thank you, glance back, etcetera.
Sand-drifts on the street empty of green,
& the man wipes off & drives.

5

10 p.m., New Delhi, July 2006.
Live marigolds for a small shy show.
The Year of Chicken Fever.
Dust knocks against glass;
trees so brittle a breeze keels them.
Against character, you are still here,
leaning into cars, learning to please,
your name green, your silence
a drift on a dirty scald.
Heat scaffolds the street & your skin.
You wipe off slick, drive old colour,
the colour of icons & rings,
say thanks as you start the car,
say bye, I'll call, whatever.

6

Leather tongued, your skin hangs
humid towers off the smoke.
Friction hiss, backseat body,
white distance pulled hard to suck.
Someone in a frenzy rolls the light
violet in the dashboard pulse,
identical information without source,
stray knowable colour, primal slick,
old clouds or grey wind or sound drip.
You laugh, your mouth worked to please.
The exits pull skin like scaffolding,
the sound of suck when his fingers stick
inside you & the man driving
says, me, excuse me, please.

7

Smoke tongue, friction hiss, all body.
Slither pulse in the dashboard light.
Information inside you stuck,
humid leather violet from your stick,
knowable primal ambient sound.
The man says excuse me and drips
old colour without clouds or grey wind.
Outside, sand drift streets without people.
Your skin scaffolding multiple trees,
old marry gold colour without exit,
high pigment number, high streets.
Scaffold sunblock factor burn.
Trees so brittle a breeze keels them.
The Year of Chicken Fever & dust

For Agha Shahid Ali

Who among us will escape the hand of water?
No cheek, no eye is dry in the land of water.

Bolt tight the windows, the wind is fierce tonight.
Read the collected works, unsigned, of water.

Tomorrow, my love, we'll walk our bereaved city.
We'll see what the streets understand of water.

Last night the moon said your love would abide.
How wet are your eyes with the brand of water!

Someone is singing a widower's song in Malayalam.
I'm reaching for your hair, beribboned, of water.

When the starlings return to the streets of Manhattan,
Wake me. Till then am I a man, unmanned, of water.

In the Almanac of Rain you will find all my lines,
Each rhyme and refrain, each ampersand of water.

Jeet, meet Shahid, your guide to the future.
He'll teach you to play a baby grand of water.

2007

Locked in your head with English,
you number a beat that feeds the day,
but a system exists to deny English
to you who know no tongue but English.
The word with which you order time
is a kindness, a gift made in English
from your years in a house with English.
At dawn, someone's voice calls your name
for pleasure in the sound of your name,
its meaning plain, but only in English,
in a page that passes from hand to hand
and lifts like a bird, white, from a hand.

You hold to the world an empty hand
that fills with the shapes of English.
In your city, someone's prayerful hand
ignites a street, a square with light. A hand
that waved to you—was it yesterday?—
returns as a chalk outline of a hand.
What will you read in the lines of a hand
outstretched, with nothing, not even time,
inscribed in it? It says too much is time-
bound, love, luck, the seasons, the hand
you deal, are dealt—fixed as your name
on a stone, and the dates below the name.

Cruelty without reason, in whose old name
some reject the lovely arm, the hand-
some face, the unfamiliar name,
and learn to husband evil in god's name,
holds nothing dear for me or you. *English
spoken here* was the promise near your name.
You could've been The Man With No Name
for the way you drifted through your day-
dream which transformed each holiday

into mythic disaster, something name-
less that struck a town in the pages of *Time*,
and would do so again, time after time.

Misfortune works in cycles beyond time.
These meanings are contingent, the name
attached to an object, divisions of time,
the fragrance in a room of dead time.
Unchangeable and correct, the minute-hand,
its formal drop—Greenwich Mean Time—
that tells you nothing will turn back time
or tragedy. You, solo chewer of English,
spit your lines of broken English
to God who's busy and keeps no time.
You'll remember stray details of the day,
'I'm my own ghost, I too died today.'

In a damaged city, you take each day
express to the top, where a custodian, Time,
places no bulwarks against the day
his work fails to separate night from day,
forgetting from love, silence from a name.
What sets the week in motion each Monday
sets you off on your own *Groundhog Day*,
stuck on repeat, unable to lift a hand
to change or delay the blood-black hand-
made conclusion. The outlines of day
blur, and the actors have no English.
There's no help for us but in English.

So I speak to you now only in English.
I'm walking with you, hand in hand,
hoping you remember, this is my name,
here's where we met, this is the time
we had together, an hour and a day.

A Home for the Holidays

       Blessed are the dead,
especially when it rains, and much more blessed
—in all weather—are we, the warm and fed.
Young Bones divides his time and sets his clocks
among the living too, but we're better dressed,
       we don't live in a box,
and we have more to lose (in a word, all).
A fall, a flu, a fool, and the earth unlocks
its treasures, its deep tableaus, its boredom.
Up here, we don't know we're incidental,
       we can believe in some
things. The way you gulp your days like coffee,
two at a time, and find yourself a hum
to call your own, well, dear Mr Chicken,
you may as well grab the special offer,
       use it while it's open,
don't let your addiction to punching time
blind you to the gains of indecision.
A habit is a bad habit, like day-
light and the need for it. Better to mime
       the morning away,
better to mix another vodka-lime
and think about the things you'll say today.

ENGLISH (2004)

Praise for *English*

'Jeet Thayil's work is, quite simply, the genuine article. I shake, vigorously, his hand.'

Thomas Lux

'I revel in Jeet Thayil's poetry. He seems to be one of the most contemporary writers I know, and contemporary precisely because he has such command of the poetic and historical past, and because his invented language has such depth, archeological richness, and reality. The staying power here and the imaginative strength, which allows the soul to be forever balanced on the cusp of the inner and outer worlds, are nothing short of remarkable.'

Vijay Seshadri

'Thayil's poems refract his vibrant, unique and far-flung life experience through the prism of a tremendous lyric intellect. The result is a fantastic realism that will haunt me forever. Thayil's *English* first spices a transcendent command of diverse registers of literary and colloquial speech with certain sprung local talk, but then melts all that into an infinitely focused and inventive, personal and emotional idiolect, delivered in one of the most unforgettable voices of our time. He is a master of the knockout lyric punchline. Some of his poems made me cry, which is rare.'

Philip Nikolayev

I
MOVEABLE

About the Author

Born in a hamlet near the southern Him-
alayas, the author's youth was spent in,
and under, the twin shadows of madness
and avalanche. 'Of the two, loony tunes
are much more better,' he was told by
his long-suffering Ma, who, ten months
pregnant ('he was not wanting to come out,
poor baba'), married her father's long-lost
brother. Born on honeymoon, the author's
his mother's first cousin, his father's great
nephew, and his step-sister's loving, ah,
husband, though that comes a little later.
Right about now it's time to switch view-
points to the man of the mommy himself.

Title for an imaginary sequel:
Ishmael, Fishmeal, call me what you want,
just call me, okay? Stop. Go syllabics:
One only I recall of all the fish-
like faces of my wives, oh, one. I swear
now, on the moment's talk I am allowed,
swear her hair and every pore was adored
by light. I'd wake to the smell of guavas
poached in milk, the sound of peacocks adance
in dawn-soaked hanging gardens, and she, a
season with wings. Not the youngest, the most
beautiful, or the most fertile, but she
is the one I remember now, countries
away from the plangent peril of Hind,
the rainy country I was king of once.

I do not ask for much. Keep your silver,
give me instead something simple, a field
of blue, say, or green, or a square foot of
red, the colour bleeding at the edges,
held together by happenstance and pins,
and let the good owl Severn be my guide.
He, no I, was walking in Colaba,
on a day late in the monsoon, looking
for *The Times of Bombay-not-Mumbai* and
a smoke of O and the next thing we know
I'm standing on Sixth, watching ruin, with
a handful of rain and a prophecy,
no idea in my head what next to do,
say, be, or think, or any thing, except

the taste of ash in the pulverized air,
this morning by the Flatiron, drifting up-
town, just before the savage winter of
2001, everything settled
at last, the star anise folded between
my eyes saying, I am not of your race.

*'Truth is for years I suffered whenever
I ate,'* my father told me as I stepped
into this weird new world, *'pork, not bacon
but pork,'* and he nodded at the baby
back ribs and vindaloo-rice on my plate.
'But dad,' I said, 'but Nissim, but Dom, but
TJS, how will I walk in the world
and not eat of its food? How will I walk?'
I asked my sweet old father, asking him
to help me with this last thing, this last time.
*'You keep / kosher to show your love for the
void,'* Gerald replied. I knew he meant *word,
love for the word*, is what he meant, I know.
The author now lives in New York City.

Moveable

All right I admit it, I am struggling, I am.
Naming the sacred is not a job you take
lightly, not, that is, if you want to live
to any half-ripe sort of age. Until 1989
we were frequent companions. I visited
you, entertained you—in Bombay behind
the Byculla zoo—and, merely a month later,
in HK, we lived in Repulse Bay on a junk.
After that my memory becomes hazier
with pain. Was it you I spent a month with
in Chiang Mai, smoking opium in a stilt-
house with the chief and his daughters?
We had so much money then, it was as if
we were on vacation from real life forever.
I remember: I am bringing home goodies
—imported coffee, cigarettes, geraniums
in a jar. I am sitting on a scooter,
you are in the sidecar, laughing in tongues.
Who would have guessed the disaster
in store, or how rarely you would appear
in the decade of denial? I am in my thirties,
shirtless, a baby elephant's head grows
out of my shoulders, I carry a beer-
belly and shades. My mother is bathing.
I am on guard duty, which I enjoy.
As my Asiatic time came to a close
you and I grew reckless, racing borrowed
toys through the streets of ghost towns
patrolled by soldiers, priests, guard-dogs,
and always the inscrutable face and
lotus feet of the first Godman, Sri Sri
Baba Ba. On the airplane we sat
by the aisle—sharing drinks, magazines,
maps to the world—measuring our journey
in statute miles. At JFK you scurried

off for coffee. 'Back in a mo,' you said,
'and remember, yaar, the nail in your head
is moveable. So move it why don't you?'
In the fall of 2001, I do, I walk
from Roosevelt Station to a basement room
in Jackson Heights, past Hindi movie-houses,
cut-rate travel agents, kabab halls, suit-
sari shops, paan-DVD parlours, psychics.
You, I am beginning to suspect, are not here.

Skewed

I am on a street, already *somewhere*—
say downtown, say Perry and Hudson,
where Hart Crane lived for a summer
and Dylan Thomas fell, as if into sleep.
I am poor. I am no tourist. I am hitching
my cargos past the angular bones in my hip.
I wear a black and white scarf at my throat,
folded not knotted, my coat buttoned up,
and I know I am ready as ever I will be
for America, or I will be ready once I
get myself a hat, it being winter and all.
I walk stiff-legged towards Christopher St.,
see too many blocks between 10th and 11th,
and find that the city is skewed, sweetly,
for those who see the skyline or bridge
in this poem's wavy right hand margin.
My regenerate heart pumps like a bird,
floating on auto, ever unwilling to land.

Afloat, the Immigrant Martyr Elect

I step off the plane,
bob like flotsam
above the scene
of future martyrdom.

The world machine
—*I know*—waits to greet me
with blood tests, green
ink, spy cameras, ID.

Nobody is there. I
do not understand.
I know how to fly,
not how to land.

In Quetta, Queens,
and West Asia, PA,
I found my cousins.
They shouted all day,

wept together at night.
Weekends spent
in study, we ate
only halal and lent-

ils. For weeks on end
I heard no word
of English spoken
but 'New York!'

Light falls, stars drown.
Grief rises, wearing feathers.
In this way we are one,
We die together.

It Wasn't Until the Lawyer Told Me I

could not leave that it got to me. I was
struck so deep by the notion of home
lost, I could barely breathe or sleep or dream.
I'd come out of the subway in one of those
Manhattan canyons and for a moment see
the stretch of street between Sree Liquors
and the left turn to the sea where a Russian
freighter ran aground in suburban Bombay.
The lawyer said I'd let things drift so far
that now I'd have to pay the price, she said,
berating me. All I could do was agree,
for I had let everything drift as I stepped
through my new life, dozy on downers
and meds. I thought of the life I left behind
and it seemed like some sort of blessing
suddenly, everything I tried so hard to escape.
I remembered waking every morning, nothing
on my mind but the tick of the lampman's
needle on the stem, telling me to suck
quickly at the pipe, before the pellet burned.
The sick-sweet grace of opium, like love
enveloping me, as the unhurried orange light
lit up the room in the late afternoon and I
picked up my books, my change, my shoes,
took a bus to the city where my wife waited
to feed me, the day's mail and newspapers folded
by my plate, as if I'd been working hard all day,
and the lawyer on the phone from Miami said
I'd waited too long, the price would be steep,
and I said yes, it is steep, the price, steep indeed.

The Man Who Married Water

lived alone with his love,
together they churned or quiet
lay. His wife and he,
solitaries, rode the river to the
sea. Every tributary
led to her, to water.
Though his wife be jealousy,
she was water, she watched with
eyes of rain as the whales'
ancient terrain cracked,
the old routes now
led elsewhere, to a great
head stunned by land,
bound by sand. He
found himself drowned.

The man who married fire
married everything.
He married desire,
filled the room
with his striving.
(He *was* consumed.)

The man
    who married
        air, saw

himself fall
    into a spiral,
        his hands

gripped tight
    on the wheel
        of a plane

hurtling
    down, a
        plane that

was
    not
        there.

Only he who married
earth was unsurprised.

September 10, 2001

How much harder it is to speak
when I have spent the whole day silent.
I would like to stop someone,
leave my room in the evening and stop
someone, a man without hope,
or a woman bent double, as if she were
searching the sidewalk for gems caught in
the cracks, and I would tell her that each
of us walks with the same impossible burden,
knowing that only the stars will last—
she will listen to me, hear what I say
and go on her way, bent over as before,
never looking up at the approaching sky.

II
SHAPESHIFTER

How to Be a Girl

Tiny cherubs of joy paddle the air.
Must I mention their preposterous wings?
No: I sit. I pull the door shut,
the cubicle expands like feathers.

The girl walks in, hesitates.
I watch her stop her shoes next door,
the bottoms of her frayed blue jeans.
(I'm trying not to make a sound.)

She bends down, places paper
on the seat, carefully sits.
Her shoes face forward,
the jeans fall to her feet.

I listen, then, to the sound
of fabric falling down
to the floor of the stall.
The girl is gone.

I pull on her jeans,
shoes, underwear. Again,
the sound of God's snake hissing:
sudden breasts on my chest.

Outwards I soften.
Stubble falls from my face.
A cleft of African violet
swells with the sea.

My lifeline lengthens.
My seat fills out.
I feel my smell change—spicy,
mysterious, so sweet I gag for fear.

How to Be a Toad

Take three fresh spores
with a dram of rum,
hold it on your tongue

for longish moments.
Pack all thoughts of gold
in a small leather case

the size of a sapphire.
Say to yourself repeatedly,
'I'll never again be beautiful.'

How to Be a Leaf

Hold your breath until
you are God's green thoughts.
Stop eating,

air will suffice for food.
Water is another matter:
the skin absorbs moisture,

eyes adjust,
limbs grow inward.
Conjugate patience.

Worship women and trees.

How to Be a Horse

Know the nostril,
all power gathers there.
Inflate yours until the blood sings.

You will need all your training
to be horse, not ass.
It is a thin crossing

perilous to the absent-minded
and the estranged of heart.
Avoid all latitudes.

How to Be a Crow

Learn to name the animals
—Stinking, Babbling, Breedy,
Querulous, Maddened, and Jet.

Usurp the duties of God.
Why not?
This is what poets do.

As for crow,
kill colour,
turn black.

How to Be a Bandicoot

Assume dominance
over the underworld.
Your enemies are legion

—eat them.
Eat everything.
You must build your strength,

change will surely come.
Your eyes are red legends.
Your name is Adam.

How to Be a Krait

This one is easy,
let your grief take over.
Enjoy salt.

Forget the rest.
When your skin falls off,
sere as bone,

laugh out loud.
That is the first thing. The second:
Avoid the mongoose.

III
ACHE

Fool and Flea

Dearly beloved
we are gathered here
to join together
this fool and this flea
in holy matrimony.

Fool will sing,
flea will suck.
Fool will work,
flea will pluck.
Both will learn

the virtue of obedience.
Fool will give up his freedom.
Flea will give up
whatever chance
she may have had

at happiness.
Both will die.
Fool first.
Flea so full
she'll burst.

The Air There is Crowded

I

Here we stand, steps away
from our first home.
Look closely at the way

the picture takes shape: three rooms,
two faces, a patch of lawn.
We are smiling. You will cram

the house with red Kohima rugs,
Jaipur cotton, scrolled iron,
a rocking chair, greenery, jazz:

your signature in a corner
of each shining
room. Look again: I trace your

face in the ransacked air, and
trawl the hall for a sign
that once I lived here not alone.

II

He stands by the bed where lately they lay
an instant, strangers joined by name.
The morning rush hushed now and still,
an absence too vast for thought to fill.

He stops to stare at a space on the wall,
remembers nothing but farewells too soon.
Idly swung, the cradle swings still.
Wondering, he roams from room to room.

The post-its are tales too tall to tell,

the kitchen ghosts mostly want out.
What was it brought on this rout?
He takes a last look around: all's well.

Botero's Pear

A painted pear hangs by her bed,
too-ripe belly flesh I knead.
My job's to cleave like rock
to the bruises of her back.

She stares at her Botero pear,
each blemish glowing with flavour.
A red worm wriggles the skin, and I
wriggle too, blind in my turn, supine.

The blue hour stills my hand and breath,
frees my brain past pain's last fever,
to the time of the fallen, *la ora de la ora,*
this hour and the hour of our death.

An egg of pear-shaped disclosure
fills my mouth, in a Bowery room,
with the one aphasic word
left at last to Baudelaire—*Crenom!*

Villanelle with a Line from Baudelaire

Obsidian his eyes in the neon light,
blinded by vision—a car, her hair.
Listen, love, how soft walks the night

in silver anklets, how timely the right
it grants us: to make ourselves better.
Obsidian his eyes in the neon light.

Driving away, her wires pulled tight,
she watches him fade from her mirror.
She'll walk, and listen to the night.

How well he talked, blazing with insight.
How did fervour not convince her?
Obsidian his eyes in the neon light.

Ungainly, unkempt, a dodo in flight,
he finds himself saying, I am truer.
Listen, his love loves the night.

And he? Calmer, it takes all his might
to shamble on as love's lost lover.
Obsidian his eyes in the neon light.
Listen, love, how soft walks the night.

There's a Chinese Wall Between Us

Smoke seep, tire hiss,
motor roar—
a din that does not cease.

Next door, a dour
man, ardent
in dark glasses, snores,

a glottal stop and start.
I wait for
you to climb out

of the slumber
that divides
us. You shudder,

slip into the tide;
your hair
upswept as you ride.

Your feet syncopate their
sleepwalk
rhythms. Your bare

hands pare dreams, invoke
breasts;
your thighs unlock.

I watch your hands at rest,
blind
baby animals in aspect.

How small they seem
in flight
from the giant in your dream.

Sailor's Log

Tacked to the dark
swell of her back,

I wake up dreaming.
Morning

spills like milk
across the floor. Birds build

fractured arpeggios;
my friends in chaos.

They speak
the secret words I work to keep

safe in my chest.
Why say the rest?

I long to be
misery,

my race obscure in a crowded sea,
shipwrecked, dizzy,

free.

Psalm Secular

When you I taste
god awakes
from a century's
sleep or murder.
I fold my hands,
press your blessings
to my head.

I kneel abed,
mouth small praises
where thy thighs
collide. I bow, arise.
Soon the sun
will do the same,
arise and bow.

I take two pears
from the Gauguin bowl,
shine them with your slip.
We eat sweet and fast.
Juice flecks our lips.
'Gravid!' I shout,
for the poor joy of it.

And you? Laughing,
my name in your eyes,
you cry one word.
The moon that hangs
above the street
on a silver thread
lifts its skirt to dance.

IV
THE GENESIS GODOWN

For every word has its marrow in the
English tongue for order and for delight.
Christopher Smart, 'Jubilate Agno', lines 584–599

English

Here I stand for the seventh and last time
by a sign that says, 'Welcome to Bombay.'
It could be any great city—crammed,
brimming with rage and suffrage—
I would be ruined still by syntax, the risk
and worry of word committed to stone.
English fills my right hand, silence my left.

Walking to the dabbawallah's shop
for a copper wristbone to replace the one
I wore out, humming with knowledge
stretched as far as it can go and further,
to give you now seven plums
that range across the seven colours
of wisdom, each with its own worm, each
called by its own loving name: Alias,

Stretch, Gall, Fear, Blister, Scrum, Mankind.
Ripe with history, residual
vigour and the sounds of battle,
not your figures of good and evil
but players on no-man's land
between experience lived and written:
you are etched in water, sculpted in wind
unless remade by the transfiguring hand.

All else is vanity and play, death-before-
and death-after-life. So pick your worm
carefully, look for flavour and vitality,
place in a full-bore metal thimble and
drop into ear or mouth. Ignore pain,
all discomfort is momentary,
possibly false. Move on to the kingdom
before you. If you want the dung

beetle, you must take all six—rampant
males (one dead of a sensualist's disease)—
and place them near your navel, where
they like to meet. As for me, by the city's
north walls, near the ladies' latrine,
I set a flotilla of baby striders
afloat on the sticky green water.

I fill my hat, take with me as many
as I can. Their joyous humming lifts
us aloft, airborne like our brothers,
the giant flying beetles of my home.
Smearing honey on my skin, I let them
drink me to their fill. They are alive
and well; they deserve to be happy.

After all, this is where I live, a place
they too have chosen.
I see them now waiting for a gesture. I
raise my fist and provide. I see my winged,
scaled, armoured siblings slap their genitals
once more with rage and decry the terrible
litanies of St Thomas, '*Mary, you too may
become a living spirit resembling males.*

*For every woman who makes herself male
will enter the Kingdom of Heaven.*' I take
the female dung beetle by her tiny hand

and follow Her Daintiness into the best room.
She is too awed to speak, too cowed to say
thank you, but she will lead us, I know,
fearless in God's crazy teeming gardens.

Summer

Colour the horned snail
red for the fire that begets it, keep it
safe from the sun that robs it,
colour its home white on white
(make it rich enough to fill in
for the absence of shade trees,
conversation, or hope for comfort),
fold the light above it, and stand
beside your emissaries,
the Saguaro, the Joshua, the sea
without end, or pity, or water,
until something clicks inside us like light;
we are here to sing the permanent
cadence of sand, here am I, ready.

Moon

Arched and pitched to light tight as a talking drum,
I move nocturnal systems of poverty and frenzy,
my single stare lets lovers share the sweet hands,
Dionysian currents, purple in subordinate air,
fill this miser's ward with silver coins of plenty;
I am Anarch, mistress and master of great Stonehenge,
flocks of firefly bearers hum the midnight's song
in tongues unknown to babbling man, Babylon, Babel:
call me by my name, though my name's a braid,
my name is moon, *it is not*, I am moon, *I am not*,
my sly eye's wanton twin is fat, white, everywhere;
I am turned by water, returned by the crescent,
quartered and corrected by the many-maned ocean—
when you stumble home on unlit roads and fields
of burnt-out resin, the nod-poppies of oblivion,
fix your eyes upon my spilt wide-open single one,
know that above you, always above, I wait to speak
of star or wave—*what else?*—the red robes of birth,
the passing craze of infancy; answer me no answer,
no one say no thing, let word be light be Cyclops,
I am your place in the comfort-making hearth,
cell of bone and runic parchment, papyrus pap
and driftwood, last dance of twilight before
the trumpets shrill, I am your sister, your mother
moon am I, confidante of couches robed in analytic
cloth, bedlamite, friend to traitor and debauch,
whore of god, condoled by hellion or monarch,
I am this I am, moon-made, remade, maker of moon.

Monsoon

Oyster-tongue, mangrove maw, the river's raw
sour breath, its moist air encumbered with mud,
mad with waiting and grief, ready now to shed
upwards its uncoiling of earth's dry dirt-thirst,
long-held summer vertigoes of the ringing light
when the safe-sided contours of Kerala blur
to dazed stillness before the grand chaos of wind,
every fur and scurry must stop, pause in a pose of
praises and prayer;
then in the small rain something fierce stirs
the river's grim, single-minded currents, furrowed
by history's keel, trawled by the spinning sleepers
fallen to its revolving arms—even the changeful
river knows this change will turn vast systems
awry—and the true rain begins: random power
endowed with shower of bounty, whips wind,
shreds vine, cracks bark, mangosteen, jackfruit,
slaps the baby palm, uproots lemon, tapioca,
flattens the cowering tufts of pineapple, and douses
the world in torrents of self-cycled water, maddened
by sea-rhythm and pounding heartless drudge
for unclocked hours, a constant torment of deluge
slow on the green land, the river, the annihilated air
—snakeholes flooded, monkey and woodpecker
mute, cats made fearful, cattle clustered—
the houses funnel a rush of worried water,
water plumes through its own wet world, fierce
in its dream of water, and water made flesh of water,
a perfect craze of water, the mother of water,
of water creatures born from the water in this line.

Dawn

Surrounded by revellers of starlight and sea-scrum,
our green-grown house fits snug inside the music,
the trance-sparked triple-headed serpents,
phosphorescent sea monsters on shore to dance
and regard the slowed time, motion stilled to a stop;
the hiss and slap of surf remain, all other sound
drowned, and always above us the absence of light,
the stilled air a mirror of our geologic need—
false dawn, still unseen, little more than a notion,
waved away as some collective hallucination—
then true brightness begins
to bleed across the sky a circumscribed swell of bass,
cryptic the beat of Eden's demoniac percussionist,
pulse-strumming contrarian whose enjambments
thicken the air to a glowing bubble of firelight, who
drives the dawn to a prodigious flowering, counter-
points the crack of carrion crow's first call
and the bone engine of the day's new castanet;
when morning's swift machine overtakes the stars,
scatters around us the mercy of brightness,
this oracular dawn reveals us for what we are:
a heaving tribe of bodies blessed at the feast,
as if each were a bowstring plucked and left to ring
some signature tune, a new and tonic metronome
more varied than the multi-modal juggling of the sea:
uncontrolled, speed-made, fearful, wide-eyed, weeping,
we grapple with the permanence of ecstasy and time,
our arms upraised in praise for love's racing anapaests,
for this frenzied mythmaking, for the mystic-riven
morning's holy page of dawn, spoken in a song.

Winter

Waking in white light I stepped out of the house
you share with husband and child, left you sleeping,
the House of Unnamed Dread open above you—
stumbled past sequoia and oak, five hundred years
of gardening gathered toward a cold disclosure
half-understood in the apocryphal fall, its off-
season secret of sieved light waiting to be shared,
up where the delicate sister of air exhales a tune
so strange it appropriates every stir and spill,
the curved Haar of mind-made Doune—you wake
in the House of Grape to desolations of the dead;
morning's slow-moving secret, already spread,
intones monochrome inversion of tree-bole, stone,
approximates hue and tone, the tumult of sunlight,
irregular pulsings of soil and dew, depleted
by the absence of filigree, suspension of colour;
no birds, no leaves, no sunshine, November,
snuffed to distant knowledge of ash, grey on grey
in a blanked-out sky, so distracted by weather
it engenders nothing, believes, invokes even less,
half-hearted promise nulled by a purifying
storm of impacted measure, tight as I hug my coat,
close to a conclusion, knowing now how it will be,
the practice of winter, its insistent soothing
and precision, estrangement's northern Omega
sealed into stone—*whose snow is this, billowing
like linen?*—so, I know and bless this ground,
the sodden seat where soon tomorrow you will sit,
unable to create a nostalgia of scent, or of me,
undone by the winter first told you on this page.

My Grandmother's Funeral

What stories you know, closed in the worm's dominion,
composed for the doomed enclosure of bone,
hair and fingernail fragment; the yellow hoops removed
from your ears and wrists. *I alone am left to tell this love.*
Light drowns in water, unseen from this church,
whitewashed on a hill in the lush south. *I alone am left.*
The congregation stands entranced, white shirts and mundus
starched, sung aloft on ancient rhythms, talismanic glow
of hymns repeated in a tongue all of us remember and nobody
understands. Some words promise an impossible redemption:
barachimo, deyvam, shudham, slomo. *My words are water.*
The evening censers pass scent of smoke
from hand to hand, from end to end of a sunlit room
where Syriac, the first figure of faith, waits with his fierce
accountings—your ally in the conundrums of Christ,
his mother, the red heart bared. *Here am I, empty of words.*
At dawn, in single beds, you and your husband lay chaste
in matrimony, a wedlock holy as hands, *I am made mute*,
perfected your children, the young dead become legend,
oversaw strict enunciation of shekels, rice and prayer.
The slow erosions of memory, tidy acres overgrown,
ungentle stripping of faces, names, ignoble disrobing
for the writer you were, grace, the first of our long line.
Crawling to eternity, alone in the one house so many sons
and daughters embarked from, *left alone to die*, you faced
the curse of longevity placed on the women of our tribe
with a wilful retrieval of dignity: the clenched refusals
of food and water, final naysaying to the sanctification
of all who lived to your great age: a life-affirming *No!*
that resounds now from the walls, fallen, of your house.

V
ACHE

The Other Thing

The other thing I want to tell you
about my grandmother is how un-
interested she was in cooking and
how powerless she felt finally
about all that chastity. She wanted
life, but the food on her table
was always the same. She told of
Sundays past, the laughing season,
she, a wife of promise, lost.
As the magistrate's bride
in a small coastal town, she took
a turn away from the feast,
to end up hungry and alone.
At the end, she found
her way to glory: she said
water was too sweet,
chocolate too spicy, it brought
tears to her eyes, nothing was right,
not salt, not bread, nothing
helped, so she stopped food. She
stopped.

Meanwhile, Over in Orissa

Sometimes I see clearly, like a man
recovering from long illness.
On this ash-grey Ash Wednesday
I try to take coffee or stand
but little things trip me up:
my face in the kitchen mirror,
a grainy image folded on the bed,
an Indian rooster's insane crowing.

Daylight is worse by far. I see
my brain's clenched fist
command the body to rise.
I stop and cannot breathe.
The book's blurred runes flap
their wings, and pyramids of gods
lift red hands, their mouths
stained with a kind of love.

What can be said about the night?
Why point out its colour and smell?
Or the Australian missionary
and his two small sons
who pray in a burning jeep.
Saffron men dance around them,
their ash-lined foreheads
tremble like crosses in the heat.

i.m. Graham Staines

The Brown Nude

On your chest a sebaceous rose,
its mystic pose enhanced
by your prayerful painter's hands

whose anointing spirals
colour the air. Crow
crawls across your eyes,

caws the evening
litany, insane.
We drop red rum

past the blackened treetops.
In the room behind us
perspective tilts,

veers to places askew.
The brown nude stands tall,
nutbrown boy-breasts

oiled in the light;
a young Tiresias,
or buff *ardhanarishvar*,

her wisdom won hard
from quarrels
with herself.

for Akbar Padamsee

The Boredom Artist

Life, said Hobbes, is nasty, brutish, and short.
He left out boring, as grim a condition as any.
His tigerish namesake's epiphany,
in 20-point captions, is a Sunday slot.
Then there's Chekhov, who, a moment ago, wrote,

The earth is beautiful, as are all God's creatures,
only one thing is not beautiful, and that is us.
Between philosopher, toy tiger, doctor, there's
a ladder of land no man claims as his.
I'll settle there with old friends, familiars:

a monkey, my famous barking birds in pairs,
and defrocked Sukhvinder, the bald brahmin bear.
Dawn, like whisky, half-lights a watery world:
all things break down to flesh, food and fear.
It's late December in Fleetwood, downstate NY,

'glorious showers, thunderclouds continue'.
My mind unwinds as the century slows,
dribbles its years to a whining close
and defunct days peddle the news.
Listen: nothing, not even love, is true.

Portrait of the Artist as an Old God

A man of 63, on his back
in a rented room,
stares at the ceiling

fan which gently cores
his vision into slices.
The sea repeats one line

he pretends not to hear.
It is already dusk,
the hour of the bat.

His hands will soon
blur in the gloom.
He lies there wide

-eyed, waiting.

Elegiac

We shake hands; yours are paper.
You tell of desecrated cities.
In the inner temple, blood-
brimmed bowls tremble at each
blow. On fine stalks of fear
your eyes
walk among drowned paddies,
boy pilots, breakfast whisky, flak.
Stories whir like flies,
only one remains untold:

how can death be not useless?
why stain the air with grief
of my own, when so much hope
persists? Priests and monkeys
chatter like static; it
sifts the fine lines that halo
your head. Ash heaves
upward. Bones fall, fill
the river, fat its oiled banks.
Your good eye sees soot

stain the sky. You salute
our awkward leave-taking.
I tried, you say,
but not enough, take
my hands and hold them,
bless me as I bless you.
Your hands
are mine. We hold a cup of air.
I drink the word 'holy'—I pray
a way to pay it forward.

for Dom Moraes

He Do the Husband

When I stuck him with the knife,
she it was who screamed
louder than a struck heif-
er. It was harder than it seemed
to see her as his wife,

and see myself half-blind
with jealousy, tied
in a double bind.
He lay down and died.
I said, Make up your mind!

But she was done
talking. She lunged
at me. I put her down
with the dirt and dung
of Babylon town.

Her scream
was loud in my ear.
I walked to my Taurus,
put it in gear,
took off to Cream

and the Hallelujah Chorus.

VI
SHAPESHIFTER

Heroination

The News—not *news*—at Nine's plenty odd:
two peacemaker warheads gone astray,
the UN building lost at sea.
Ted the evening anchor's on the nod,
taking nonstop dictation from God.

The newsroom's top brass is in rehab,
everybody else at a meeting.
The first order of business is a stab
at good cheer—dim sum to go, with Tsing-
tao and cognac—on the company tab.

Ted slurs his first question, and the next,
'What's your policy, Mr, uh, Prime,
re. distribution, storage, the perfect clime?'
The reply: 'To echo my mostly vexed
predecessor, I encourage the sublime:

more people must just say whoa!'
But the PM's got a bad feeling,
a sort of kind of sense of doom foretold;
voices in his head stutter, *told you so!*,
the studio lights set him reeling.

Next—*Dear God not now!*—a narcotic
buzz breaks out like the Chinese flu.
The sportscaster's narcoleptic,
Oprah's sympathetic,
and the weathergirl's copped one too.

Here at home, dad makes the usual noise,
'Front me two bags till the morning, boys.'
'Don't you trust him,' Mom says,
'He's ripped you off before, he'll do it
again. Give it here, you know *I'm* good for it.'

So many dilated pupils (and teachers),
twisted endorphins and pro-tease inhibitors,
the whole world's high except for me.
I alone do my job: maintain and be
the last refuge of sobriety.

The Unauthorized Autobiography of Rain

I spoke to you in many
continents, whispered
soft consonants. Why bother?

In Euro I trilled nightly
a friendly anti-rhythm,
unbound by time or rime.

What comfort this knowledge,
this old conversation?
The strip malls still call. (I let

benedictions fall on Yankee soil,
spoke—*a joke*—in tongues.)
'No English here,' I said in Siam,

heard my own forgotten name
from sources unreliable.
Nothing prepared me for monsoon.

How *prepare* for the mindless
yowls of Indic children?
My rain, they said, as if in explanation.

Am not, I said, as if in reply.

Ophelia

I touch myself.
I kiss you.
You see nothing.

My dreams turn:
barking Pierrots,
copulations mysterioso.

Last night a bird spoke...
*Look for the light,
it will come from the north,*

...lies.
I long for ooze,
frogspawn,

bright ring of algae
round my throat.

Inventory

Body remembers blood beating
    in the womb,
the proprietary touch of dream.

Body remembers brutal
    midwife's hushed job,
a damp room near the river,

incisions painting the skin,
    colour stitched down,
the unsurprising resolution.

Body remembers body, yours
    on loan, breathlessness,
the unhappy ending fulfilled.

Body remembers spawn
    battling upriver,
swelling a belly to bursting,

recalls the loud death
    threats at dawn,
crosses burning, firesmoke.

Body remembers sacred details,
    light like rum
firing up a brass spittoon.

Body remembers twin embalmers
    singing a capella,
itself unworthy of worship,

on my knees in the big house.
    Remembers, the body,
a fat lady, end as beginning.

Yet Another Mother Poem

Light careens
through my veins,
makes me whole.
I inhabit

uninhabitable days.
Small whips of rain
crack at my back,
make me holy.

Water and air
pump red squalls
of love or pain.
I fall

into your room
on frayed flat heels,
pillbox hat flat,
hands of opium tincture.

My winter breath blows
small sacraments
of air. There,
then gone.

At Kabul Zoo, the Lion

So this is fear: tracers flaring
above the pen, the fat thud

of bullets, and the bigger sound
of animals leaving our lives.

Sad-eyed, the widow elephant
saw a cluster of shells

explode her enclosure.
She screamed in narrowing circles.

Shrapnel stopped her and she dropped,
the first to fall.

Everything burned:
the tiger shrugged fire

off his shoulders.
The capuchins tried

to escape their burning tails.
The hyacinth macaws,

spoonbills and hoot owls,
flamingoes aflame...

Only the llamas stood dumb
in that madness, stupid

to the end. I envied their emptiness.
Blind in one eye,

my jaw in shreds, my mane
singed to a useless crop,

I wait for these men
to come to me.

Slumming in Bombay, Beelzebub

found himself at home. Finally, he
had a reason for lethargy.
Inert like everybody, unable to work,
he blamed the humidity.
No use to say, 'But B,
that's what this city does, man, saps you,
leaves you spent like change,
separates the dudes from the ditties.'
He was having none of it,
and then the boss arrived, unexpected,
on a Sunday.
But the boss—*now what?*—had changed.
Hard as it was to believe,
she was kind-hearted, distracted, funny,
endearing even.
The day she came to take him home
they were seen at the Hanging Gardens,
hand in hand, watching the dust bees
ride their favourite pollen machines.
It was Christmas Day, just after dawn,
the heat and humidity at peace
it seemed, and Beelzebub's boss serene.

VII
MOVEABLE

Land's End

Undermined by grace and the roaring line,
we lay ourselves open, across the cross the
seafarers climbed, past white church, tufted
wave, the endless roil of raw sea and rock.

Here Peter still teeters; not rock, not man
but Englishman, his word on water writ.
Land's end or faith's? That was your question.
Now answered, my friend, for us it's wit's end.

for Adil Jussawalla

Pashupatinath

At 'most famous Kathmandu,'
tradesmen's wives
talking shopping,

we walked past
marijuana fields
barbed neck-high

in the noon yoga;
delicate pulsings
breathing the feathers,

each ribbed leaf
the colour of
parrot skin.

A bull of beaten gold
balanced on balls
so large they dwarfed

the nesting crowds.
With hands full of money,
flowers and prayers,

our unruly lines
mobbed the priest
who slapped each supplicant

across the head,
the smaller the donation
the louder the slap.

The giant bull
sat serene,
without regard,

his gold made ordinary
in the tightening dust.

Kovalam

Saffron sun over Kovalam,
slum waters agleam, telling me
how the dream finally ended:
journey half done, we undone.

Ancestral moonlight on the tracks
took us in a rush to confess
our impossible pilgrimage.
At the station, a wayward cross.

After all that overflowing,
misery was a kind of peace.
I sat at the edge of a world,
at the end of a life, smoking

endless cork-tipped cigarettes.
The sun—fat, old, obscene—
dipped its rear into the bleak
water. Nearby, a girl's high cry.

Imaginary Homecoming

At river's edge
I cup my hands,
drink until I'm drunk,

the cool water
made sweeter
with knowledge.

This is the end
of wandering under
other skies,

the untrue north of exile.
How many camps
like this one?

Heat or cold,
or a promise of better;
we washed our thirst

with more thirst,
ready always
for weather.

Each day
brought its measure
of movement.

Cow-dung houses
abandoned, cook fires
doused, horses slaughtered.

So many rude tongues
become familiar,
we learned to keep

our own language
secret and true
to our ears.

The rank rubric
of memory,
our only constant,

and the women,
children,
exhaustion.

I let the water
wet my face, taste
spiced sun on my tongue,

woodsmoke
from the houses
on the hill.

London

The air is shut too tight, its
unoiled hinges resist use.
Every day I assay
new methods of entry,
nothing works
but a handful of pills.

The light is wrong;
slant intent
grown homicidal,
it tells us something
relevant about
responsibility,

something I do not want
to hear. It is difficult
enough to breathe,
and get this line just right.
My friends have given in to
the prevailing wind

of neglect. You can tell
by their shoes, stacked
against the brute
passage of time.
The rubber soles are coded:
these shoes will last

longer than us.
Then there's the night
sweats, the chill wind
come straight off the moon,
aiming at me
its Jabberwock garrulity.

You get no rest here,
nobody does.
Even the rain wants to talk
of insomnia or shopping,
which, it says repeatedly,
is better than sex.

The river arches its scaly back,
inviting kin from above,
the mirror-river in the sky,
to join the monochrome
festivity, the tedious
feast, the permanent fun.

Time now to move,
for the motion and ease
of movement, everything
moving without meaning
toward the water
where once we lived.

Doune

He stops,
stunned by sun;
too bright for any country
other than
his own blighted one.

No mist, no Haar
follows him with mute intent.
Wherever he goes
the tropics go too.
Until one blear morning,

laid low in the highlands,
he wakes in a child's room
guarded by tiny animals
—a monkey with a tail
long as a length of string,

a giraffe, seven bears,
droop-eared puppies—
and a multi-coloured ball of wool;
he wakes, I say, with fragments
from the memory museum,

unable to recall who he is,
or where he may be.
He keeps his eyes tightly closed,
hoping to hold on
to this pleasing amnesia;

he cannot remember
when last he felt so cheerful.
When he steps into morning,
there's a chill mist
thin as strands of cotton:

blank, absent, without meaning,
a landscape untouched
by history or memory,
a place whose weather
matches his own.

Hongkong, 1997

What's he doing on this creaking barge,
tethered to a wintry island sea? What
does he hope to find huddled under
wet tarpaulin? Unseen objects knock
against the hull. He's pared it down—all
of it—to this unlikely cohesion
of metal and wood, afloat on a whim
of candlelight, the moon clanging on water.
My God thou hast shriven me, he says
aloud. *Yes, Lord, thou hast taken from me
all vanity and surcease. Bone-weary,
I beg recompense. I wait to be plucked
and played but all night thy terrible hands
push against the stern.* Morning brings no
clarity but a pasty haze like the moon's,
though colder. Nothing's certain in this
kind of light. The old woman who rows him
to shore wears a veiled umbrella hat. Her
wide and unforgiving face is as impassive
as December on the salt South China Sea.

APOCALYPSO (1997)

Praise for *Apocalypso*

'Here is weighty and daring poetry... It is not brutal encounters that you get, for Thayil is not out to shock. Each poem is handled delicately, like expensive crystal being held up to the light. His talent lies in working the gold out of the mundane and the workaday. He wrings out poetry and "legitimate sorrows" from "prize pettinesses" which the soul is heir to, finds "the sublime and the vacant" "both ridiculous at one go." Only the whore's "sadness tells the truth"... There are some poems like "Working Girl" or "Apocalypso" which should speedily become anthology pieces so that they can live on for another 50 years. (Poems live longer in anthologies.) Magic hovers over life and landscape in some of the poems. One strange dawn in Ajmer, he looks back at his life to suddenly find "No trace of habitation". Sometimes his verse gives the impression of being "waited upon by ghosts", with a lovesick boy on top of the stairs finding that "Everything takes on the fearful clarity of dream". Thayil moves on boundaries, on hyphens that bridge different states of minds, in the spaces between dream and reality.'

Keki Daruwalla in Outlook

I

Working Girl

1

Outside, evening trembles on its axis,
mustard oil steams the air; all of Asia's
captured there, in musk-red exhalations
of hair, the very same head of hair
Baudelaire once shook like a kerchief,
now lies outspread, black sea parted,
divided by red, offering holy solace
in a tumbledown bed, from here to hear
the womb wound's bloodied rite of birth,
sprung rhythm from the female earth.

On the skinflint street a red lamp burns.
Just bathed, dressed in her best, she returns
to her place by the door and the thing she
knows best of all: to love is to wait.

2

Come hither, she says in any language,
spitting in her palms, wetting herself,
slapping her thighs like a slender
wrestler, bored expanse of flesh agog,
vast on the raised platform of her bed,
squat on the raised platform of her sex,
no doubt in her mind of victory.

I'm thinking of the real thing on
some late-night sports channel from Japan.
They're superstars, these big men, bigger
than the Pope, knotted in G-string diapers,

monster babies bred only to fight,
like this woman bred only to fuck.
The announcer introduces Kawakabuto,
whose game, he says, is 'disciplined violence
with a sure requirement of intelligence and speed.'
There's some pawing of the ground, a false start
or two, a spilling of salt, spit, sometimes blood.
They scowl and slap their thighs, circle and feint,
then, with a thump heard throughout the arena,
ram into each other locked at the neck until one
topples over like a felled bullock. You can hear
the women gasping, they won't leave a dry
seat in the house. These men die young.

The Quilt

I'm making a patchwork quilt
of many unsayable colours,
one for every man I've loved.
When it's done I'll wrap it around me,
she said, I'll wrap it tightly round,
then I'll lay me down
and I won't get up again.
It's the hardness of men's bodies
I like, she said, giving mine the quick
one-two. It's the only thing
keeps me going through the thick
and the thin, especially the thin.
Fully dressed on her unmade bed,
I lit a quick black cigarette, making in
my head a perfectly worded confession.

Ballerina

I thought, the minute I saw her,
mutant fatso baby ballerina,

steps fluted like a stork,
fleet feet fluttering. Not.

(The music crests and bobs,
as it does when I'm on my jobs.)

Drunken ballerina minces
madly, offers up her slender graces.

Nobody wants
a dancer broken from the dance,

a pointy thing, stark
raving at the dark.

Later, ballerina legs
thrash, crimson hosannas bubble her lips

and the stained blue eyes carom
as I move about the room.

Apocalypso

North American angels die young,
cheeks hollow from blowing out forest
fires, marks of past beauty still
visible on earlobe, nipple, bicep, nostril,
skinny always, bearded sometimes, haunted by
waking dreams of the Mall of All America.
Tiny spoons or half-razors dangling
from neck chains, American angels live
alone with their pets.

Rosy-cheeked, skulls shaved to the skin,
beery border-line booze-hounds,
British angels are strictly segregated,
not by gender but colour and accent,
white is wary of brown, brown of black,
black of yellow, yellow of white, and so,
perfectly, on. They will deny to the end
that they're racist, past it, pissed. The talk is
of the good old days. Only sunshine can
reduce them to silence.

Angels in Spain are endangered, the few that
remain are transfixed in the glare of meat-
packed freezer trucks pounding the highway to
Madrid or Toledo. Spanish angels love to
eat and drink and spend their inheritance wisely.
In France, the angels live only in Paris,
or are headed there, or come from there; are wary
of the rain, for they know French rain can kill;
do not die of tuberculosis; see no value
in misery, poetry or poverty. Absinthe they
can take or leave.

Slavery binds Asian angels in a new impoverished
brotherhood, gaunt angels, permanently deferred,

who speak, dream, write and kill in English,
language of their once and future masters. Life
is good as long as there's television and tourism,
and if there isn't, well, then, life can be altered
organically, chemically, life can be recycled,
and home wired to the dish that cannot feed.
Dona Paulita, meanwhile, caresses the bundle
wriggling her arms: Pierre, the pink and sacred
baby pig squealing to be fed. Asian
angels go hungry.

Betray Me Before I Betray You

Everybody betrays everybody, you said
somebody said. I thought of the countless
betrayals our combined flesh had tolled,
residual jealousies marking the way, past

forgotten monuments to heartbreak. Robed
forefathers sing the Aramaic song,
nothing prepares you for the slaughter
in store there by the cigarette machine.

Prize pettinesses the soul's heir to, yet
capable of the most legitimate sorrows,
the sublime and the vacant ridiculous,
both at one go. Your sadness tells the truth.

Pushkin Knew Heaven

(A Place Where Nothing Happens)

The first hint of first light
brings me instantly awake.

You stir gently in your sleep,
dig yourself deeper into bed,
my pillow over your head.

The newspaper at the door is cold
from its journey across the city. I
make coffee, as I do each morning,
scan the headlines, sip from the cup,
look out at the quiet street.

There it is, all of it, and it's nothing
short of a miracle.

If there is such a thing as happiness,
it is this.

Hello Goodbye

Driving home, desperate,
the chill air gathered round
my head, where I live now.
Robin Trower powered me on.

This at the hour before dawn,
I still high from your presence.
Now, sun hinting, I wade
through dream to eight o'clock.

Hello is fine, but there's nothing
like goodbye to make the man
come truly alive. Look at him
there, finally aware of morning.

He must climb into his box to sleep.

His Twin is No Hypocrite

His twin brother, Depression,
in the iron lung,
has no room for doubt
or the various
pettinesses littering the room.
He's lingering,
(malingering, some would say)
because he can.
If you tell him to say when
he'll reply in Japanese,
madadayo: No, not yet.

Strapped down and trapped
in a white bed in a white room,
his twin doesn't complain or tell a lie.
He does not grab at the nurses.
His thought is clean, tight as a drum,
altogether in a purer space.
His twin is the better man.

Where This One Came From

1

Tonight she walks in moonlight,
reaching for something she cannot name,
a twist of muscle maybe, maybe a knot inside.

She will not promenade tonight,
she will skulk beside you if you're lucky.
(Skulk is a word stolen from the future.)

She's sober as fuck, no? No, not as fuck,
sober as stone cold jelly, staring for a face,
her own, in the eyes of johns and jimmies.

(I think I meant jaans and jaanus,
considering which side of the hemisphere.)
'Vampire junkie from hell,' private joke

she's too distracted to note.
She finds a cheap hotel, vestibule
lit by a single yellow bulb.

2

On the bed, she spreads her need
open like a pack of cards.
You take your pick, but it's wrong, homes.

She examines the four-chambered room,
the heart & comes to a slow decision:
the penthouse. Pay later/never.

She opens wide legs & arms,
gives herself completely, comes
in the sick blue colours of withdrawal.

Poem is as poem does & is done by.
Now watch poem sleep the pure slumber
of children, drunks, fools. By first light

she will vanish, leaving you, shadow.

Vertigo

The day he stands at the top of the stairs
waiting for something to break or yield,
plosives detonate his lips, hard consonants
rattle and burp, the air bright with images of
shit, dead dogs, burnt bald Butoh gods.
Corruption of ancestors staggers his breath
with ecstasy or bliss, some blessed foretaste
of death. The banister keeps him upright—
no oblivion's allowed, only good boys deserve
favour. In his head, the familiar descent is a
special danger, a full tumble fully foreseen.
Then, swift images of a city in the south,
sea light, temples, ragged trees. Trapped
on the top step, the day takes on the fearful
clarity of dream. He's probably done for.

The Adulteress Addresses Herself

Fat moon in a smudged sky,
God's unblinking night-time eye.

I touch your face with mine,
condemning us both,
setting off flocks of white
birds in my blood.

On the wheel sparks fly.
The knife sharpens the stone.

One Morning at the Cattle Fair

Eastbound he rode, earthbound
on passenger trains that stopped
at all stations and then some,

made good time
through the badlands,
dacoit country now tamed.

One strange dawn in Ajmer,
he woke by a mist-made river,
found himself neighbour to herds of
elephant and buffalo, and
newer horses never ridden.

At water's edge he looked
backward over his life and found
no trace of habitation.

Genesis Partner

1

Choking on air, like a mermaid on land,
she hears her name in several languages,
in the house severed by history,

by the misshapen hand and cloven foot
of time. Twin burghers these, time and his wicked
twin, built to rot the fruit on your bough,

to shove into meaty mouths the dough.
She sits at head of table, waited on by ghosts.
Ghosts attend her passing, to the left of her

the angry ghost of her father's father,
to her right, a familiar shape redeems itself
from the night, the ghost of her most recent self.

2

Violent journeyman of two wretched sons.
One is travel, the other death. Both stink
Of promises brashly made, already broken.

Travel's the winged vagrant, moulting begun,
prodigal replacement, some minutes younger.
Death is the captain, oar captain, colder
of course, but bolder too, and a laugh a minute.

Wedding Picture

Late at night, by my side,
You are the loneliest ranger.
Dreams wormhole the future,
Show you how to stop this life.

Birds drop, skies lighten.
Round the cape of no hope
We awake, you wife, I husband,
Our ship a room of wet rope.

Some mornings, the moon holds
The wall like a slim white lizard.
Your fingers read the world's
Book of Hours, backward.

Bees stop, flowers die,
Grief takes its human shape.
These are the signs we make
To know we are alive.

II

Self-Portrait

Unhappiness is a kind of yoga, he tells himself
each morning, a breath meditation; besides,
do you want to be happy or do you want to write?
When he lifts saucepan to stove, images atone
forever in his hands. Ghosts of celebrations past
throw themselves lemming-like into the meagre
flame, each small act attended by a host of demons,
friendly and not. The world is code, smoke signals the
dead have left us to decipher, knowing we cannot.
At nightfall, exhausted by toil, he falls deep into the
dreamless light changes, the dead or dying sea.
A mountain moves and nobody notices. The world
is old and set in its ways, and K. is saying, Of course
there's hope, there's always hope, but not for us.

This Mortal

Here are the talking monkey men
breaking news of a pink infection.
How small it seems,
how local a transmission,
how foolish to call it 'the transformation
of society as we know it.' More pertinent
to ask: How will we be true to one
another when the world only seems to gleam,
when intent
trumps biology, is trumped in turn by the bent,
each a glory, each a misery, become
in the end
nothing but a stratagem
to temper the beast, nothing certain
but the sweet foreknowledge of loss?

Bitter knowledge, tight response:
Why be true, when everything returns
to dust and meaninglessness?
I could say none of this matters
but the truth is it does,
each demise
matters so much it hurts
the mouth into words
that ride the river some call Remorse.
I think of you sometimes when the hours
slow into nights like this,
when the memory of repose
wells and drips into a history of catheters,
bed pans, pethidine, tears,
and you turn up in my dreams, your eyes
wide open, your hair singed, or sparse,
your lips stitched to a single seam.

Tentative Like Us

Mornings opaque with possibility,
every kind of strange weather at the edge of
day, behind the crack of window
pane, rain trickling upwards,
smoked light, monsoon rain, wet
heat, all the seasons, all at the same
time, as if undecided what next to wear,
the weather thought to try out its
entire repertoire, three seasons in a day.

Other People's Deaths

1

John Berryman jumped into the frozen
Mississippi, a terminal case of love
deferred, suicide son of a suicide.
Before the jump he wrote: 'I didn't and
I didn't sharpen the Spanish blade.'

Think of him cutting his throat as he
jumps, making doubly certain, the ice
too thick to let him drown, but hard
enough for the fall to kill, or John
hacking his way through the river,
darkening now with his fastidiousness,
his scholarly ways, poor Pussycat.

2

Delmore in a broke hotel,
attacked by the volatile
poet's heart he carried
for just that purpose, felled
near the elevator, taking out trash,
alone by then, wives, friends,
mistresses driven away by
paranoia and the peculiar
Delmorean delusion that
collapsed his life around him.
The desk clerk found him,
he'd tried to tear off his clothes.
The body lay unrecognized
for three days. A writer's
joke: there were no readers of
modern poetry at the morgue.

3

'The litanies of perfect health interest me not at all.
Give me instead the nihilism of the will.'

He followed his own perfect nihilism to
the end of the earth, or to Mexico.
A year in the Guggenheim sun,
fellowship run aground, he jumped
a ship bound for home, for cold
weather, sex misery, intercontinental
debt. He had, always, a foot in the sea.
Voyages and islands underlie his lines, and
that's where he went in the end,
after breakfast, to forever be lost at sea.

The breakfast is crucial, see him calling
room service for everything on the menu.
Hart Crane, all of thirty-three, the same
age as crucified Christ, ordering bacon,
three eggs, pancakes, maple syrup on the
side, English muffins toasted right,
butter curls, orange marmalade in pots *and*
jam, why not?, sausages and mash,
minute steak, fries, orange juice and
hot coffee, with a little spike to keep it all
down, and the waiter thinking, Boy, look at
that, man's eating like there's no tomorrow.

I, Chatterbox

Sane in my corner,
intoning news of a
cong, corpse, cock,
irradiated klong dusk.

Look me tight suit,
look me white white
shoes, boxed brilliant
head blaring seven

thousand, one hundred
one tongues, I
am bright, excited, I
feel, oh, feverish, I

soon to bark aloud.
Overtopped, whelmed to
bursting, on air button
pushed, I am first,

Oprah's on next.
There, rice birds sing,
silence rules insensate.
How much is the time?

Falling

I fell into day, walked outside,
The buildings swayed, automobiles
Barked black smoke. I walked
Past clouds to my father's house.

He was not there. Instead,
I found the doors open.
I laughed and danced away
The day until darkness fell.

At night I found the street lamps
Broken. Only one remained.
A group of boys stood under it,
Taking aim with perfect stones.

I ran to them, my brothers,
Dropped everything as I ran.
Clothes, ID, keys all fell.
Nothing left in the moonlight but me.

Daft Sermon

Waking to the taste of blood
I turn the daylight on its head.
Upside-down in the heart of night,
here's austerity, distance, flight.

My own true syntax of the nerve
cell, synapse, ganglia, a trove
that syncopates my wild will
to the city's calm killing field.

Now toreador, a skintight tease,
I lie down in a special place,
I gather up the friendly dead.
I wake to the taste of blood.

The Guru

Make yourself a hollow
bamboo, he said, a tunnel
from earth to sky.

Let the breath connect your
seven round chakras,
like the holes of a bamboo flute,

seven holes for a melody
divine, he said, sipping her
seven, playing her.

Letter to America

Two in the afternoon.
You must remember it,
the most oppressive time
of day. Nothing moves,
not a leaf, not a line, not mine
in any case, nothing but the
beat of a stilled will.
I sit in shade, wife and
child lost in afternoon
naps. I'm lost
too, though not in sleep.
Scarcely lifting muscle or
eyelash, only breathing,
unwilling to disturb this heaving
oily stillness, I think of
you, my lost brother, in
your leafy groves of kodachrome.
More than distance separates us.

Blueprint, Bombay

Of a small house the master,
I stand, my two hands
held against wind and tide,
digits wide, spread to the
crease where splayed islands
lie cowed by the sea of
Araby, seven islands made
one, stitched loose at the
seams, whisper grim
nothings once of the trees, now
fodder for automobiles and
quack of executive heels—
island grows to maggot
town, leech to permanent
sun, smile of stupefied
worm, turned, never done.

No More Tears No More

It is a night like no other,
a night like all others.
He's been drinking since a little after
tea, if tea were a time
anymore. For dinner, he makes soup,
eats watching the news, then
another drink or three.
Late at night, he
takes off his clothes,
gets into bed, lets the blue
light of television
wash over him, sound
turned low. Away into the night he
swims, and wakes to rain
weeping at the windows. In the blue
square of light, a bald
man slaps himself in the
face. 'No more
tears no more,' he says
between slaps, this bald man.
Everything's clear, everything
obscure. If this is the way the world
ends, this is the way it begins.

Jacob's Circle
After Berryman

1

Standing wide-open in them thar rain,
Jacob thinks of turkeys, they die that way,
drowning the mouth.
He'd like that right now, old Jacob would,
he's had a sort of a kind of a shock.
But man's still got rocks in his jocks

& a hole where my heart used to beat.
Now that she's done for me, that
—it takes one to know one—slut.
But.
J wants to stand at the edge of the world
with this only & one girl. Hurl

at her such total love
as only he could give.
She'd have to love him back.
And then? Well, then, Jacob's gross black
soul wouldn't need her anymore.
She'd have to go.

2

Monday night Jacob maudlin at the Press Club,
he's hungry too, Hungry Angry Lonely Tired,
'Old AA saying, HALT, beware, be aware,'
so say the types who hang about here,
sucking endless beers.
Jerk-off Jacob's sinking, bub.

Descending, he pick a leaf off his arm.

A empty pack of Charms
floats across the floor.
He's drinking whisky & ice, nothing else.
There's a heaviness pressing his chest.
Insomniac Jacob later spills forth,

weak-kneed in love's O speechless night.
He's treading the boards of a pill-chilled dawn,
nudged out of bed by a hard one.
The fine young murderess in his dream
smiled as she confessed,
he nuzzled her neck, she reached for his skin,
Jacob's three selves met as they kissed.

3

Sickbed Jacob's got a lot to drink about,
but penniless too he'll instead have to think
about ev'ry daily horror.
Poor old Jake, so fallen by the by
he turns to his mind for succour.
No help there.

No flowers, no books, O not a mangy fruit.
Yacoub's treading time so raw he could weep.
He spends hours arranging the things by his bed,
putting powders and potions and tablets just right.
The more he sleeps, the more he sleeps.
(It's all in his mind.)

Now Jacob's got a visitor at last,
a dainty old crone gone soft in the head.
She looks, I'm sure, familiar.
Maybe his mother. His wife. He forgets.
Maybe somebody dead.
His eyes move from ear to ear.

Family Affair

Unnatural sounds rivet the moon,
Resound in the two-room house.
A muffled squelch and thwack,
The unmistakable fever slap.

Klansmen's silhouettes against the sun,
The four horsemen of the apocalypse
Cannot produce more dread a sound
Than elemental parental percussion.

When mother whimpers, father clamps
A broad hand across her mouth,
In silence they consummate their vows.
The extended family bears witness.

Horse Breakfast

Walking out early one morning,
past the sea in its dirty cage,
I rounded the corner to horses,
three, round a large raised pit
flowing with garbage.

Once the winged white steed
of desire, now deceased,
not mystic, hardly beast,
these Bombay horses feasted
on rot, all trace of wildness

obliterated. Ribs prominent
as their limps, manes shorn short,
abandoned to the streets,
half a step ahead of the butchers
who serve them up as mutton or beef.

Trout Fishing at Night

'Mom!' the boy yells, running into the kitchen.
'I was standing at the window and a man waved
his fish at me.' Breathing hard, tugging at
his mother's hand, he wills her to come and see,
his eyes bright with unshed tears. She wonders
at the pitch of his voice, hysteria unbroken,
and rues his world's commonplace disasters.
She lets him lead her back. Mother and son
stand by the open window in the dark.
In the house across the way, in a yellow
square of kitchen light, a shirtless man
stalks the floor, hair plastered down his head,
animated in conversation with himself.
When he stops directly in front of them,
as if he knows they're there, she clutches the boy.
A silvery trout dangles from the man's fly.

Life Lessons

People die in circles. The thing to hate
is learning what you'll have to unlearn.
'This is how to write right,'
some old poet will say. Unlearn him;
say, 'Thank you, maitre, for teaching me how
to despise.' That is a lesson worth learning.

People die heedlessly. The nuns you like
reek of hollow heaven, stubbed or frayed,
mentholated in grievance. You imagine
tremendous fornications, flying pig summers,
huge pregnancies that freeze the mind;
terminate do not germinate.
Succeed, our fathers say, or suck
eggs. People die plentifully.

Children die, predeceasing parents. Odd
that we eat birds and animals, growing
like us. Look closely at rivers, trees.
People die, that's what they do.

The Mercy Tree

Yearning for gleaming glass
And towers of sleepless steel,

He finds instead a dread
Of nature's restless flowerings.

A lush chaos, as disordered
As the random chancing of madness.

The deciding day:
Stumbling home he falls into paddy,

Wakes up bruised, more broken
Than before,

Urgently missing
The comfort of concrete.

Like my vanished neighbour,
I too know the worry of vastness.

When the clock winds down
Mark for me an urban surround,

Squalid, anonymous, free.
How much easier then

To pick up and leave
The constant currency

Of breathing for another rhythm.
This obsolete frame,

Discarded like a suit of clothes,
Will make fire, fodder or fish food,

Befriended by worms,
Milk of the mercy tree.

GEMINI (1992)

Praise for *Gemini*

'The poem is called 'A Morning Prayer'. Its iambs are English, its dark shades Baudelairean, yet right through the poem the poet remains, as all good poets must remain, himself. There's no need to look further for qualities of "Indianness". The poem's title in any case subverts the millions of morning prayers we are heir to every day and the millions more we've been heir to since Vedic times. If the poem makes us want to add a bit of mouthwash to the gargling that precedes the prayers, so be it. It means the poem has done its work. It isn't dirty work and Thayil's intention isn't to write dirty poems. Rather, his poems light up a corner of the dirty world, imbuing it with a near-holy radiance. The beautiful, uncompromising poems in this selection are an achievement and there have to be more.'

Adil Jussawalla in *Indian Review of Books*

'Thayil's verse is eloquent, flowing, metrical, visceral. He walks on the wild side. His voice is that of the present generation.'

Arshia Sattar in *The Independent*

'Thayil's world is very fleshy, but in a strange and tortuous way it is preoccupied with a sense of sin, of the image of the devil. The celebration of the flesh is gnawed at by a wracking guilt almost, or if not guilt, at least the feeling that all is not right. And yet the images of a beast-like nature pursue him relentlessly and, almost despite himself, he is fascinated, held spellbound. The poems are not imitative, they are original... That it is also a somewhat alien sensibility in this land and part of the disturbed quality of the poems and the experience—poetic and otherwise—arises out of this fact, comes out almost with the clarity of a statement in "Writing in English".'

Sudhir Sonalkar in *Debonair*

'In the watery context of modern Indian poetry, these two (JT and Vijay Nambisan) stand out like flamingoes, birds of colour and elegance. Neither is very consistent, but at their best they are superior to most of their elders... Thayil's work is sometimes flawed by his own image of himself, but at his best it is splendidly structured, both skilful and forceful... Possibly their coming is an indication that Indian poetry, after many years of striving, has at last arrived at maturity.'

Dom Moraes, from the introduction to *Gemini*

What You Are

So many babies. Creepy crawlies soaked in brine.
Wild babies. Already I see the brown stains
you will leave behind. The sick suck of lollies.

Gross, voluptuous babies leaping and falling,
a great soft mass of downy behinds. Warm
smells of baby powder, baby breath, piss.

Look at you now, sitting there like fat old Buddhas,
trying hard to hide your wrinkled baby jokes,
your gurglings and shriekings, your soft-boiled brains.

Where are your long-gone murderous moms,
flailing like coat hangers? You sit, you snort,
surrounded by bodies and soft baby laughter

and sunset noises crowding in like ghosts.
Listen, offstage we live desperate lives,
offstage we kill our own daily babies.

House of Silence

Growing up in that strange place we learned
to laugh silently for fear that laughter too loud
would bring about its own swift end.
We learned a dread of Sundays. If days had colours,
we used to say, Sunday's would be black. I learned
to sing in the dark, quietly, without joy, not
without fear, modulating my tones so he would not
hear, the big man sleeping with my mother in
the back. They sleep there still. Housebroken now,
I make token sounds in a large unnoticed hand,
gone to ground, as you said, in a loud and leprous land.

Writing in English

Muscularities of the lecture hall slow
this testimonial blood to rusted driblets
too weak to move the brain, the bed,
the passioned fist. Against foreign walls,
we reinvent our mythologies, find ourselves
newer heroes, fresher seed,
and thus sustaining, conceal the need
to build on glories of the second-hand.
Mine is a generation stuck between shores,
doubly exiled and doubly betrayed,
unscarred, uncertain, permanently afraid
of losing ourselves in nonsense words,
in memories, not ours, of better days.
The quality of thought deteriorates.

In the ruined tower we call our home
each sound rebounds on what is not there.
Our linguists' falsettos shatter on air
uselessly, echoless in the vacuum.
Throughout the attempt but lately begun
to establish our own authenticity,
we moan the fact, as also the pity,
our mother tongue is not our mother's tongue.
Mine is a generation fed on fear,
become imitations of ourselves,
playing up our various Indiannesses
for an audience that doesn't reside here.
How can it be that a new wave awaits?
The quality of speech disintegrates.

Our Lady Speaks

Like a stark staring succubus that
from one source both lives and dies,
I have come to drain you out
fastened to your mouth and thighs.

And then to batten like a worm
drawing in my nights and days,
I'll grow plump and healthy on
your blood, so red and beauteous.

When in time they find us there,
virulent, single, long-deceased,
a bored flâneur will stop to say,
Who was the sleeper, who the beast?

Fixing Father

It's time I made my peace with you, father,
soon I'll go stupid from this sly disease,
I'll be wetting myself soon, stretched out here,
begging for the swift resolution of steel.
To know you shall outlive me after all,
what a bitterness that once used to be.
Every exertion I made for a bed,
for bread or for wine, undermined by this:

never, but never, to aspire for greatness.
I remember the hot sand burning,
a hundred fingers of sand in my eyes,
hot breath of sand singing in the desert,
everywhere, anywhere the cruelties of sand,
and never calling, not aloud, for you.
I had a pride as implacable as yours,
useless to me now on this wooden perch

paying so dearly for sins never mine.
I am begging now of strangers, of fools,
charlatans all in their medicine robes
and others with butchers' hands, of women
who weep and wail at will it seems, of you.
I beg now of you, father, I forgive
these tireless eruptions of the flesh.
Even in death I do your will.

Oneroid

This woman, her milk is black,
she feeds me lying on her back.
Strange countries stop her in-betweens,
lazy with crime, softnesses, sin.

Her phallus is a Chinese pipe,
I suck upon it hollow-cheeked,
eunuched in the lamplit dark
as she sputters and spits and shrieks.

She fills me up with moving space,
I lie still and I'm gone
On nodding, neon, endless dreams.
I pine for places never seen.

Log

Here in this endlessly comforting place,
the diurnal silences swell and change,
darken the rhythms of blood or release.
Here are journeys without number or end.

Breath of the sea and faraway coastlines
take me spinning all the way to Morocco;
armpit and breast, brief sanctuaries,
put salt in my mouth pounding on the shore.

Unfolded there, ports marked in black,
suck me back into the womb whence I came
on a waterlogged crawl from belly to lap,
I founder and sink and founder again.

With Women Other Than

If my lips left stars where they touched your skin,
there would be infinities in your face
and world upon world in your absent body.

It's always in the midst of ecstasy
that I remember your face, contorted
in the many twists of a love now separate.

Passion and the appearance of passion:
it was the appearance that I possessed.
I remember all, and now with violence

undo my belt, Orion unsheathed,
each embrace a return to the earth,
back to the blackness before birth.

Goes my shuttle mind, this way and that,
skimming the ten thousand essences
soured in the wiser bodies of women.

A Morning Prayer

I squint upon the outside world
and draw into my languid gaze
cars and walls, a cat in chains,
the worn familiars of my days.

My hourglass like clockwork runs,
outdriven by its ghostly need.
Set to pound the rounded streets,
two hungers spill my sorry seed.

A certain hunger of the flesh,
the other disembodied, pure,
both softened for a moment as
the needle mounts its bite of love.

Come, sunrise, make your promise,
round it nicely for a breaking,
age my disease and harden it
into a still and living thing.

Her Song

She sings the rain in gentle ways
that call down to her from the skies
and everyone who looks her way
must stop and drop into her eyes
and stop and drop and fall down deep
and love the motions of her face
and marvel at the dance of sleep
that makes her mouth a special place.

She sings the birds into their flight
and joins them on mysterious ways
that web the world in reels of light
and move on to a special place,
to there remember dooms of flesh,
the love that calls from man and beast
and if I could but think to bless
her holiness would quell my beast.

She sings the songs that never stop
and sing back to her all the day
and though the world may dip and drop
she laughs the children on their play
and talks the plants into their bloom
and tends us through the drip of pain
so even in this whitewashed room
I learn to love and live again.

The Lover

He stands at the door,
watching her,
watching the woman swoon.
His eyes are red things,
his lips are unhinged
hurtling from doom to doom.

Up on the wall
two shadows crawl,
foretelling doom and doom.
The simpleton waits,
his fingers shake,
perhaps he's mistaken the room.

He's done this before,
stood at a door
until the sky fell from above,
but nothing can change
the shape of each pain,
he lives from love to love.

The Body's Betrayal Sung Out in Song

In blasted wastelands of the flesh
the rabid blood prowls in heat,
sluggish the beat of leper bells
driven through these empty streets.

Mine the skin that holds down fast,
mine the viscera, genitals, hair,
the ill-lit tenement of my heart
where wasted strangers stare and stare.

Their threadbare sleeves, the knives in wait,
impatient for the host who's late;
they sing and swing in for the kill.

What a moment now to die,
unheeded in the evening chill.
No dirges rung. No child to cry.

The Alcoholic at Dawn

The cup in my hand
rattles like a drum
and tells me my need.

Strange, oh strange to wake
up where the beached whale
skims the sodden sand.

Legs unsteady, undersea
eyes bleared and brimming,
I twine a blue smoke
from nose to throat,
then the quick stumble to the cupboard.

Praise the Nod

I slide in the tip,
a red flower blooms
in my glass syringe.

Your brown love
drives the blood
into my secret heart.

Then must I wait
and my cells all wait
for your touch at the base

of my spine. I smile
as the bone is breaking.

Hymn to Him

Oh take me to some quiet where
and let this frantic scratching cease.
I'm tired of the dog I bear
and all his restless tyrannies.

I'm sick to tears of his stench,
the constant maddening smell of him,
his little joys and huge torments,
his futile furtive stratagems.

Oh put him out some perfect how,
I can't support his heaviness,
his hairiness and beastliness, his howl
for food, his crave for flesh.

A Circular Song

What demon stalks this arid land,
how can you live here my poor soul?
Even the sun steps like a thief
trembling off for a deeper hole.

How can you live here my poor soul,
hedged in on all sides, fugitive betrayed,
trembling off for a deeper hole,
you cower now poisoned by hope.

Hedged in on all sides, fugitive betrayed,
reeling like a drunkard slopping his drink,
you cower now poisoned by hope
though no rope can hold, ragged soul.

Reeling like a drunkard slopping his drink,
slipping in semen, blotting his snot,
though no rope can hold, ragged soul,
slot in the slip, slip in the slot.

Slipping in semen, blotting his snot,
what demon stalks this arid land?
Slot in the slip, slip in the slot,
even the sun steps like a thief.

Acknowledgements & Notes

New and Uncollected Poems

Some of these poems have appeared in the following journals: *Fulcrum, The Caravan, The Battersea Review, The Missing Slate, Little Star, Wasafiri* and *Asia Literary Review*.

'Imaginary Translation': this is a false or imaginary translation of a poem by Ana Rossetti.

The Book of Chocolate Saints: this collection of poems was originally conceived as a book within a book, that is, a book of poems written by a character in a novel who set out to correct the historic misrepresentation of certain saints as white, not to mention blonde and blue-eyed. The collection was deleted when the novel underwent a rewrite, as novels do. The poems may or may not stand on their own. Some saints are invented, for example, Saint Santosh, Saint Nayantara and Saint Mathai; and some are not, for example, Saint Gandhi, Saint Maurice, Saint Erasmus and Saint Moses.

These Errors Are Correct

These poems first appeared in the following publications:

Fulcrum, 'The Cook's Tale', 'A Home for the Holidays', 'Superpower', 'Dear Heptanesia', 'The Penitent', 'Quiet and Concerned with Provenance', 'In the City of Insomnia', 'After', 'The Miniature', 'The Annotated Gita', 'My Paris', 'The Art of Seduction', 'New Year, Goa', 'You Are Here', 'The Origin of Remorse'; *Mudfish*, 'To Baudelaire'; *Salt Hill*, 'A Cure,' 'Late Vespers at the Hudson'; *Kavya Bharati*, 'The Opposite of Nostalgia'; *Catamaran*, 'After Brodsky'; *Drunken Boat*, 'Spiritus Mundi,'; 'Flight,' 'A History of Religion'; *Mirage/Period(ical)*, 'The Two Thousands'; *The Journal of Postcolonial Writing*, 'Letter from a Mughal Emperor, 2006'; *Contemporary Voices from the East: An Anthology of Poems*, 'Spiritus Mundi'; *Softblow*, 'To Baudelaire,' 'The Two Thousands,' 'The Penitent,' 'New Year, Goa'; *The Cortland Review*, 'The Sonneteer'; *Salt*, 'Malayalam's Ghazal,' 'The New Island'; *Wasafiri*, 'For Agha Shahid Ali,' 'The Eye,' 'Poem with Prediction'.

'The Cook's Tale' was nominated for a Pushcart Prize.

My thanks to Stephen Sturgeon for the title of this book.

Some of the poems were written and revised during a residency at the Bellagio Center's Villa Serbelloni on Lake Como.

'Not Remembering': the poem's speaker is an aspiring amnesiac, but his recall of detail—particularly when it comes to gossip and art arcana—is accurate.

The line 'Naranja estaba el colour de su vestido, / then silk blue' is a partial translation into Spanish of the Charles Mingus title 'Orange was the colour of her dress, then silk blue.'

'A bird readies the soul // and moves it to tenderness' is a quotation from St Teresa of Ávila.

'Premonition': the sonnet sequence grew out of a collaborative postcard project with the writers of the group 7 Carmine.

In Sonnet 4, the line 'like shining from shook foil' is from Gerard Manley Hopkins's 'God's Grandeur'.

'Flowers for a Parijat': 'Than this, no worse', alludes to the following lines from Hopkins:

> No worst, there is none. Pitched past pitch of grief,
> More pangs will, schooled at forepangs, wilder wring.

'Letter from a Mughal Emperor, 2006': much of the action in this poem—and some of the language—is taken from *The Baburnama: Memoirs of Babur, Prince and Emperor* in Wheeler M. Thackston's translation of 1996 and Annette Beveridge's translation of 1922.

'The Sonneteer': a (slightly) fictionalized version of the life of the poet Dom Moraes; some of the incidents recounted here are true, though the sum of the poem is not. Moraes's own version of these events is available in *My Son's Father: An Autobiography* (1968). Henrietta Moraes's version appears in *Henrietta* (1994).

'Taking a Line for a Walk': from Paul Klee, 'Drawing is like taking a line for a walk.'

'After Brodsky': the poem refers, throughout, to Joseph Brodsky's 1971 poem 'For E. R.' (also known as 'A second Christmas by the Shore') from his *Selected Poems*. It is not a translation as much as a pastiche.

English

Some of these poems—sometimes in different versions—appeared in the following publications: *Fulcrum, Rattapallax, Verse,* 7 *Carmine, lyric, Poetry Wales, The Independent, Stand, Agenda, London Magazine, Lines Review, BBC, Nth Position; tehelka.com, Post-Postmodern Review, Times of India, Art India, Biblio, Indian Express* and *Kavya Bharati*, among others.

'At Kabul Zoo, The Lion,' 'The Genesis Godown: I. English, IV. Monsoon, and VII. My Grandmother's Funeral', 'The Shapeshifter's Inventory', 'English', and 'Hongkong, 1997' appeared in *Reasons for Belonging: Fourteen Contemporary Indian Poets* edited by Ranjit Hoskote.

'English': the lines in italics quote *The Gospel According to Thomas*, from the Gnostic Papyri in the Coptic Museum at Old Cairo, Vol. I (Cairo, 1956), pl. 80, line 10—pl. 99, line 28. The Gnostic Library consists of thirteen volumes found in 1945 in Nag Hamadi (Upper Egypt), most likely dating from the fourth century AD.

'The Genesis Godown: VI. Winter': this poem owes a line to Thomas Hood.

'He Do the Husband': the poem takes its title from a section of T. S. Eliot's original manuscript for *The Waste Land*. Ezra Pound deleted the passage and it was never subsequently used.

'The Other Thing': my thanks to Gerald Stern, who suggested the opening lines of this poem.

'About the Author': the lines in italics quote from Gerald Stern's 'Hot Dog', Part III, p. 71, *Odd Mercy*. There is a reference to Gerald (Stern) in the poem's last stanza. It refers also to Nissim (Ezekiel) and Dom (Moraes), the high modernists of Indian poetry. TJS (George) is my father.

Apocalypso

Some of these poems first appeared in the *Poetry Review, Rialto, Wasafiri, Lines Review, Illustrated Weekly of India, Biblio, Fantasy, Indian Post, Sunday Mid-day, Free Press Journal of India, Literature Alive, Kavya Bharati, Independent* and were broadcast on All India Radio and Doordarshan.

'Ballerina' owes a phrase to Yeats.

'Pushkin Knew Heaven (A Place Where Nothing Happens)' owes its title in part to the Talking Heads.

'Mortal Construct': originally constructed as a parable for the time of AIDS. There is a response in the poem to a question posed by Matthew Arnold in 'Dover Beach'.

'Jacob's Circle': the sequence is patterned after John Berryman's formal invention in *The Dream Songs*, that is, poems of three rhymed six-line stanzas that somehow evoke the sonnet.

Index of first lines

'About suffering they were never wrong,	15
A long time ago or this morning,	134
A man of 63, on his back	202
A painted pear hangs by her bed,	184
All are agreed he was sly about his needs.	16
All over those bland, continuous	39
All right I admit it, I am struggling, I am.	165
Always born in some close	122
Among the categories of disorder	149
Among the trees of the city,	77
Annie chops her notebook	97
Arched and pitched to light tight as a talking drum,	193
Around the room, the names I did not know	144
As starlight, as ash or rain,	29
Asp I took into my vein,	135
Assume dominance	179
At 'most famous Kathmandu,'	215
At 48, the youngest	107
At river's edge	217
Because he's old and unsure,	72
Being interested in travel	84
Blessed are the dead,	159
Body remembers blood beating	209
Born in a hamlet near the southern Him-	163
Choking on air, like a mermaid on land,	242
Colour the horned snail	192
could not leave that it got to me. I was	169
de Porres; born in Lima,	61
Dearly beloved	181
Driving home, desperate,	235
Eastbound he rode, earthbound	241
Everybody betrays everybody, you said	233
Everything that lives, will live	87
Everything, everyone goes into that mouth.	152
Fat moon in a smudged sky,	240

Five floors above the traffic of Bombay	146
Forget the sea, let it fade.	82
found himself at home. Finally, he	213
From this window,	18
From those to whom much is given	136
Give up your pen—you won't make a rhyme tonight.	73
Gone and *gone* doesn't mean a thing—	74
Good to hear from you tonight on the worldwide web.	44
Growing up in that strange place we learned	268
He stands at the door,	277
He stops,	221
He was stacking branches for firewood in neat rows. He wore a	37
Her wheatish complexion lit by the sun,	112
Here are the talking monkey men	245
Here I am for a second Christmas,	150
Here I stand for the seventh and last time	189
Here in this endlessly comforting place,	273
Here we stand, steps away	182
His twin brother, Depression,	236
Hold your breath until	176
How can I make amends to you	133
How can we be sure he was among us,	100
How did we know to go, to obey?	141
How much harder it is to speak	172
I am on a street, already *somewhere*—	167
I am over you at last, in Mexico City,	88
I buried the snowshoes.	111
I fell into day, walked outside,	250
I like you in your new, whitewashed houses	145
I lost the house. I lost the way home.	67
I set out as soon as we made landfall. I took only water, my	33
I should have ducked	102
I slide in the tip,	280
I spoke to you in many	207
I squint upon the outside world	275
I step off the plane,	168
I thought, the minute I saw her,	230

I touch myself.	208
I was born in the Christian South	92
I was famous, I won the Hawthornden prize.	110
I'm back where my life and I parted ways.	143
I'm making a patchwork quilt	229
I'm trying to forget	147
If my lips left stars where they touched your skin,	274
If you marry me	125
1. In a red and blue swatch of sky	24
In blasted wastelands of the flesh	278
In the end it took so little to do us in:	96
In the hands of the priest	75
is experienced in the collection	7
It is a night like no other,	255
It was stacked against us from the start.	12
It wasn't rain, but giant	101
It's going to take one line or six	47
It's time I made my peace with you, father,	271
John Berryman jumped into the frozen	247
Know the nostril,	177
Late at night, by my side,	243
Leap tall buildings in a single bound? Forget	109
Learn to name the animals	178
1. Let us govern those who undertake the telling of stories.	14
Let's say you're not opposed to the ghost	28
Life, said Hobbes, is nasty, brutish, and short.	201
Light careens	210
Like a stark staring succubus that	270
Like someone who comes home late	10
Listen! Someone's saying a prayer in Malayalam.	91
lived alone with his love,	170
Locked in your head with English,	157
Lord, it's time for summer to end.	42
Make yourself a hollow	252
Maybe in the slow, reptilian Seine,	126
Miracle—no other word for it—	131
'Mom!' the boy yells, running into the kitchen.	260

Mornings opaque with possibility,	246
mother of Rooturaj the ulcerous,	50
Muscularities of the lecture hall slow	269
Never easy, the way the body falls	105
North American angels die young,	231
Nothing here's worth a tick.	94
Objects in that room reflected nothing	113
Obsidian his eyes in the neon light,	185
Of a small house the master,	254
of Byculla, started his career	53
of Darfur; stolen	60
of Egypt; born in Coma	59
of Hippo; educated son of a pagan	58
of Porbunder; in darker South Africa,	54
of small fry, pi-dogs & romancers;	49
of tailors, convenor of abusants;	51
of varied climes in the same location;	52
Oh take me to some quiet where	281
On the third month	132
On your chest, a sebaceous rose,	200
Once, carried by the rains of September,	115
or Erasmo, or Rushmore, or Elmo;	56
or Moritz, or Moorish, or Mauritius,	55
or Sinter Klaas, in the Dutch vernacular;	62
Out of the depths, O Lord, I cry to thee:	22
Outside, evening trembles on its axis,	227
Oyster-tongue, mangrove maw, the river's raw	194
People die in circles. The thing to hate	261
Poem of no cleverness—	129
Saffron sun over Kovalam,	216
Sane in my corner,	249
She sings the rain in gentle ways	276
She woke early and read a sura about the Day of Terrors,	41
Smoke seep, tire hiss,	186
So many babies. Creepy crawlies soaked in brine.	267
So this is fear: tracers flaring	211
Some are cute and old,	27

Sometimes I see clearly, like a man	199
Standing wide-open in them thar rain,	256
Start with fish.	117
Still time for the grief, the note and its revelation years into the	138
Strips of rain, white	128
Sunday holds its head	76
Surrounded by revellers of starlight and sea-scrum,	195
Tacked to the dark	187
Take three fresh spores	175
The air is shut too tight, its	219
the Astonishing, climbed trees & buildings;	48
The bees of summer sail the avenues	139
The black cars huddle on the street and	6
the Black; Ethiopian servant,	57
The Consolations of Age	19
The cripple and his Inner Riches,	127
The cup in my hand	279
The day he stands at the top of the stairs	239
The first episode	45
The first hint of first light	234
the future was as they said it would be	13
The Hermans dance a white concertina	4
The Lord is my shepherd, I shall not want.	23
The lynx with the deep pink eyes	11
The midnight's cataracts whiten,	148
The moon endures its own revolving,	40
The News—not *news*—at Nine's plenty odd:	205
1. The organism's structure centres exclusively on eating	32
The other thing I want to tell you	198
the Penitent; or, the Harlot of Antioch,	63
The yak is allowed because one sustains many.	121
There's a parade in the white	137
They bar us from the republic	106
They were fighting fish, no question about it, so brilliantly	35
This one is easy,	180
This woman, her milk is black,	272
Tiny cherubs of joy paddle the air.	173

Collected Poems 291

To leave me on the F train, a lone	79
to lick the meat from each other's bones	80
To our bodies, expanding, numberless, slow,	81
To see if I'd still be here,	78
Tonight she walks in moonlight,	237
Town of ghosts, where I or some other breathes	8
Two in the afternoon.	253
Two reasons I like writing sonnets—	20
Undermined by grace and the roaring line,	214
Unhappiness is a kind of yoga, he tells himself	244
Unnatural sounds rivet the moon,	258
Waking in white light I stepped out of the house	196
Waking to the taste of blood	251
Walking out early one morning,	259
We shake hands; yours are paper.	203
What are you doing, what improvised thing?	9
What demon stalks this arid land,	282
What stories you know, closed in the worm's dominion,	197
What was the point of it? The stoned	89
What's he doing on this creaking barge,	223
Whatever it's about it's not about	103
When I stuck him with the knife,	204
When it rains, the dead descend, you appear,	83
When the flooding in the basement got worse	151
When you I taste	188
When you leave you'll take what I remember of love.	26
When you stop on Market Street	114
Who among us will escape the hand of water?	156
Who has done this?	99
Who will speak to the fish in their shiver?	116
Yearning for gleaming glass	262
You can beg all you want,	130
you remember cities never seen	21
Your lips go from sunny side to suicide in a single click.	3
Your name is different there, it has no hook	86